D0403083

"*Mass Casualties* finds the truth behind the most recent propaganda—the small stories, the base commonality of human nature revealed in war. A purely personal and timely story, moving from black comedy to a sun-baked depression, anchored with unsparing honesty."

Samuel Sheridan
Author of *A Fighter's Heart: One Man's Journey Through the World of Fighting*

"Anthony's painful account of his time at war is at times difficult to read. This coming-of-age war memoir details the very gut-wrenching journey he takes into manhood in the backdrop of grueling combat. His voice is unique and deserves to be heard."

David Bellavia
Co-Founder of Vets For Freedom; Medal of Honor and Distinguished Service Cross Nominee; Author of *House to House: An Epic Memoir of War*

"Michael Anthony's candid narrative of his service in Iraq is far removed from the glamorized picture of military life that has become a staple of our mass media. Instead, we are confronted with a world of men and women psychologically strained to the breaking point. You will share his sense of disillusionment after reading this eye-opening memoir."

David Livingstone Smith, PhD
Author of *The Most Dangerous Animal: Human Nature and the Origins of War*

"*Mass Casualties* is a raw, vivid look at the realities behind the daily news about American soldiers overseas. You will think differently about news from Iraq and Afghanistan after reading this book."

James Fallows
Author of *Blind into Baghdad: America's War in Iraq*

"Glossy recruitment brochures tell one story. This book tells another. Beyond the slick fantasies promoted by the Pentagon and the euphemisms reported by the news media, *Mass Casualties* offers readers an account of war that cuts against the mythical grain."

Norman Solomon
Author of *War Made Easy: How Presidents and Pundits Keep Spinning Us to Death*

"The human cost of war is excessive, as this harsh but thoroughly absorbing book by Michael Anthony reveals. It's a riveting account of life within the pitch of battle, giving us—his grateful readers—the feel of this war, its dreadful tensions, its horror, its absurdity. *Mass Casualties* is an important book, and it deserves wide attention."

Jay Parini
Author of *Promised Land: Thirteen Books That Changed America*

"There are plenty of books about war, usually featuring the trigger-pullers who directly engage the enemy. *Mass Casualties* looks at war from a different angle, from those who try to save the wounded and dying. Make no mistake: Their war is just as difficult. Michael Anthony has captured the intensity of the OR, the crushing fatigue of shift duty, and the inevitable clash of personalities that are part of any military unit. It's a great read for anyone who wants to see the horror of war from a new perspective."

Tom Neven
Marine Corps Veteran; Author of *On the Frontline*

"The full story of the Iraq War remains to be written, but the first-hand accounts of young people who were there can help us begin to try and make sense of what is often taken as a senseless conflict. Amidst the politics and economics of warfare there are individuals struggling to survive, both physically and emotionally. The least we can do is listen to their stories with genuine empathy and an open mind, as we seek pathways from war toward peace."

Randall Amster, JD, PhD
Executive Director of the Peace & Justice Studies Association

"A moving account of a young soldier's story. This deeply personal memoir gives voice to the countless soldiers we have yet to hear from and never will."

Yvonne Latty
Author of *In Conflict: Iraq War Veterans Speak Out On Duty, Loss, and the Fight to Stay Alive*

"*Mass Casualties* is a raw and humorous account of Army medics dodging harm from mortars and the military bureaucracy. Michael Anthony gives us a gripping memoir of a young soldier trapped in a world of incompetence and hypocrisy that results from a total failure of leadership. This insider's view of what really happens in an operating room full of combat casualties and the effect it has on the caregivers is eye-opening. Our wounded warriors and those who care for them deserve far better."

Colonel Steven O'Hern
Author of *The Intelligence Wars: Lessons from Baghdad*

"Michael Anthony writes in the tradition of Joseph Heller and Richard Hooker, demystifying the theater of war and revealing our soldiers to be all-too-human figures—comic and petty, but sometimes heroic and tragic."

Marc Folkoff
Author of *Poems from Guantanamo: The Detainees Speak*

"This isn't a portrait of the typical army experience in Iraq; this is one young man's perspective on what happens when poor leadership fails the challenge of command. Michael Anthony calls it like he saw it, refusing platitudes of the virtuous American soldier. If only Vonnegut or Heller had material like this."

Alex Vernon
Author of *Arms and the Self: War, the Military, and Autobiographical Writing*

"Michael Anthony's candid journal of his tour in Iraq offers a vivid sense of day-to-day life in a war-zone medical unit. He enriches our understanding of the variety of ways—sanctioned and unsanctioned, honorable and sordid—our occupying army deals with boredom, fear, frustration, and loneliness."

Christian G. Appy
Author of *Patriots: The Vietnam War Remembered from All Sides*

"SPC Anthony's authentic journal opens our eyes to the corrosive effect of the military mindset on human sensibilities. This is the unadulterated grit of history, in the here-and-now."

Ray Raphael
Historian; Author of *Founders: The People Who Brought You a Nation*

"*Mass Casualties* is a true-to-life exposé of the absurdity of the war in Iraq. Anthony lays bare the hyper-reality of American knowingless-ness about Iraq, and captures the day-to-day insanity of the war. *Mass Casualties* is a must-read for patriot Americans concerned with the U.S. global empire and the undisclosed truths of the Iraq occupation."

Peter Phillips
Professor of Sociology and Director of Project Censored,
Sonoma State University

"SPC Michael Anthony channels *Baghdad ER*, *Catch-22*, *M*A*S*H*, and *Lord of the Flies* as he narrates his dark, entertaining, and tragic journey through war. A thoughtful, candid, and mesmerizing glimpse into the enigmatic world of a U.S. Army combat support hospital."

David J. Danelo
Former Marines Captain; Purple Heart Recipient and Iraq War Veteran;
Author of *Blood Stripes: The Grunt's View of the War in Iraq*

"Michael Anthony's book *Mass Casualties* is unique and important. Readers of this incredible book will never look at war or its aftermath in quite the same way again."

Stanley Krippner, PhD
Coauthor of *Haunted by Combat: Understanding PTSD in War Veterans*

"From traumatic injuries to anthrax shots, Michael Anthony has cap-tured in intricate detail life in a combat-zone operating room. As someone who's done two tours myself, even I learned an incredible amount."

Brandon R. Friedman
Iraq Veteran; Author of *The War I Always Wanted: The Illusion of Glory and the Reality of War*

"A scathing, satirical, and often shocking trip through "the other war" in Iraq—the war within the U.S. Army, and within a soldier's soul. Michael Anthony's memoir is the perfect antidote for anyone who would glorify war or its impact on warriors. He has penned his generation's M*A*S*H, with echoes of Catch-22 and Hunter Thompson's Fear and Loathing sagas.

Charles Jones
Journalist in the Iraq War; Author of Red, White or Yellow?: The Media and the Military at War in Iraq

"Soldiers are witnesses to chaos and carnage, and there is a false belief that they should recover from what they have seen and done, and have had done to them. A dark secret about war is that it seldom builds character. Michael Anthony has written an honest book that is both sobering and relevant."

Donald Anderson
Editor of "War, Literature & the Arts," an international journal of the humanities; Author of When War Becomes Personal: Soldiers' Accounts from the Civil War to Iraq

"Compelling. Frank. Funny. Disturbing. Michael Anthony loses his innocence in a slow-motion train wreck you can't help but watch. Mass Casualties opens up a brand new conversation on the War in Iraq."

Damon DiMarco
Author of Heart of War: Soldiers' Voices from the Front Lines of Iraq

"If you are afraid of the TRUTH don't read this book. SPC Michael Anthony's personal experience of WAR has no censor. Reading his book is a journey into the battlefields of death, sex, and the loss of his innocence."

Lawrence Winters
Vietnam Veteran; Author of The Making and Un-making of a Marine

"*Mass Casualties* is a terrific story of war, emergency medicine, and the men and women who suffer to treat wounded soldiers and civilians. On top of this, he tells the story beautifully, managing to convey both the chaos and the boredom of life in a combat zone."

John Merson
Vietnam Veteran; Author of *War Lessons*

"A raw and uncompromising account of one Army medic's experience in Iraq."

Tim Pritchard
Journalist; Author of *Ambush Alley: The Most Extraordinary Battle of the Iraq War*

"A heart-wrenching tale of the war in Iraq imbued with a sense of outrage, but judicious in its descriptions of those who tried to change things."

Robert K. Brigham
Professor of History and International Relations;
Author of *Iraq, Vietnam, and the Limits of American Power*

MASS CASUALTIES

A YOUNG MEDIC'S TRUE STORY OF **DEATH,** **DECEPTION, AND DISH'ONOR** IN IRAQ

SPC MICHAEL ANTHONY

Aadamsmedia

Avon, Massachusetts

Copyright © 2009 by Michael Ruehrwein
All rights reserved.
This book, or parts thereof, may not be reproduced in any
form without permission from the publisher; exceptions are
made for brief excerpts used in published reviews.

"Reintegration" reprinted with permission from Samuel W. Tarr.

Published by
Adams Media, a division of F+W Media, Inc.
57 Littlefield Street, Avon, MA 02322. U.S.A.
www.adamsmedia.com

ISBN 10: 1-4405-0183-1
ISBN 13: 978-1-4405-0183-8

Printed in the United States of America.

J   I   H   G   F   E   D   C   B   A

Library of Congress Cataloging-in-Publication Data
is available from the publisher.

This publication is designed to provide accurate and authoritative information with regard to the subject matter covered. It is sold with the understanding that the publisher is not engaged in rendering legal, accounting, or other
professional advice. If legal advice or other expert assistance is required, the
services of a competent professional person should be sought.
    —From a *Declaration of Principles* jointly adopted by a Committee of the
American Bar Association and a Committee of Publishers and Associations

Many of the designations used by manufacturers and sellers to distinguish
their product are claimed as trademarks. Where those designations appear
in this book and Adams Media was aware of a trademark claim, the designations have been printed with initial capital letters.

This book is available at quantity discounts for bulk purchases.
For information, please call 1-800-289-0963.

To the men and women of my unit in Iraq:
It no longer matters how we got here,
only where we go from here.

The stories contained herein represent one man's journey in Iraq; they do not represent any organization or person other than the author. Names, identities, and small facets of stories have been changed to supply anonymity for the characters involved. Although everything written is based on Michael Anthony's experiences while in Iraq—based on his own recollection and journal entries—they do not represent word-for-word documentation; instead they are retold as if the reader were in the room with the author as he explains the stories.

Everything that follows has been verified by Anthony and several fellow soldiers who served with him while in Iraq.

ACKNOWLEDGMENTS

I would like to thank all of the great people at Adams Media for their hard work and dedication to my book. A big thanks to my editor Andrea Norville, Karen Cooper, Beth Gissinger, Paula Munier, Wendy Simard, Frank Rivera, and Bob Shuman. Thanks to CR, MR, and ET—for letting me get away with not cleaning the house while I wrote.

REINTEGRATION

Straighten up, it's alright
You can look me in the eyes
True, I am an American soldier
Serving this country, called home
This does not mean
I've humiliated prisoners
Burnt villages
Or killed any babies,
I am just like you.

There was a time
When I felt the same
That this uniform meant something
I reached for it
And all it offered
Only to be led into war
By mercenaries—hopeless and blind

Now that my tour is over
Let me slip back into the world
That I left behind.
We are now, simply neighbors
Occupying the same tenement
With the rats in the basement
And the leaking roof.

So please, save your parade
I've got no use for it now
I was just, doing my job

Samuel W. Tarr

PROLOGUE

"You are going to war! It is no longer a question of if you are going to go, but a question of when. Look around! In a few years, or even a few months, several of you will be dead. Some of you will be severely wounded or so badly mutilated that your own mother can't stand the sight of you. And for the real unlucky ones, you will come home so emotionally disfigured that you wish you had died over there."

It's week seven of basic training and my drill sergeant is preparing us for war, and the possibility that we might soon be dead. Eighteen years old and I am preparing myself to die.

MONTH 7

"THIS IS THE TIME WHEN TIME WHEN LOGIC AND REASON NEED TO OVERRIDE EMOTION."

WEEK 1, DAY 1, MOSUL, IRAQ

0900 HOURS, AIRFIELD

Loaded with gear—a three-pound helmet, thirty-pound armored vest, eight-pound weapon, and thirty-pound rucksack—we're running. There are four hundred of us from thirty-seven different states across the United States. All of us have been brought together to run the 178th Combat Support Hospital. In the plane we were briefed about how the bad guys love to bomb the airfield even though we're in Kurd territory, supposedly our allies.

A man is coming through; I tear my gaze from the sky. I automatically salute him, a colonel.

"What are you doing?"

The colonel glares right at me.

"Are you crazy?" Denti elbows me hard. "They want to take out the higher-ups, not the low ones on the totem pole."

It's been almost two years since I've graduated basic training and was told I'd be going to war. Since then, I've finished a year of college and four months of pre-deployment training at Fort McCoy in Wisconsin. Now, here I am in Iraq with a small, thick, Greek man from Colorado named Denti. He acts like such a kid even though he's twenty-three, which makes him only three years older than me. Denti's always been a storyteller and I quickly learned to never believe *anything* he says, including the fact that he was a pimp, drug dealer, gang member, and a weightlifting power-lifter—he says he only joined the Army because he wanted to get away from the hectic lifestyle.

"If there was a sniper nearby and he saw you salute an officer, he'd know exactly who to kill. Didn't you ever watch *Forrest* fucking *Gump*?!" Denti yells, as he lights a cigarette.

The sky is yellow, orange, and brown scratched together—not like the blue sky in Boston. An Iraqi man is staring at us; I see him: He wears a black and white turban, which I know means he's been to Mecca. I'm not sure if I've seen skin tone like his before; it's golden auburn. I notice that it's the same color as the buildings, and the buildings are the same color as the sand blowing in my face. They're the same color as the sky. I think that if I were fifty feet away and there was a pile of sand, a building, and a naked Iraqi man, I wouldn't be able to differentiate between them. They all look like they belong together: the tiny buildings, the man with a face that's tired, the sand, the sky, and the sun.

In the distance is a dome, clearly American made; it doesn't belong at all. We're not supposed to be here either? It's the northern part of the country, a hot spot in Iraq. The enemy is looking for the officers, the leaders. Don't salute in a war zone.

Lesson learned.

WEEK 1, DAY 2, IRAQ

0730 HOURS, OR

I've got a belly full of bacon and eggs and I'm about to have my arms elbow deep in someone's stomach. I feel anxiety build up, but I know I can't show it. Someone's life is going to be in my hands. Not just a patient, but someone's son, daughter, brother, sister, mother, or father—in my hands. The worst part of surgery isn't the surgery itself, it's before the surgery when you're waiting and thinking. Thinking about what if I mess up, what if the patient dies and it's my fault. This is the time when logic and reason need to override emotion. Emotion can lead to death while reason and logic lead to life. If during surgery I let fear take over, I will become distracted and the patient will die, but if I *will* myself to stop thinking and let my muscle memory take over, the muscle memory that was programmed into me during my OR (operating room) schooling, then I know everything will be okay. Willing myself to stop feeling is nearly impossible, though. My body is full of emotions swirling around inside, with each one fighting to be the strongest. The fear hits, then the anxiety, then the nervousness. I stand there, taking it all in. I am paralyzed but I know what I must do. I close my eyes and breathe slowly and deeply. With the exhale, I tell myself that I don't care if the patient dies. I tell myself that emotions are pointless and that nothing matters. I open my eyes back up and the fear, anxiety, and nervousness are gone. I am blank. I feel nothing, and this is how it has to be.

I look over at Reto. He's scared; I can see it in his eyes. Although I've only known him for a few months, already he's a best friend. Reto, short for Retoller; he's from rural Maine, and to my surprise he *did* grow up with indoor plumbing. Not the redneck I expected him to be, he's actually a good-looking guy who could have been a model if it weren't for the fact that he's practically blind and wears quarter-inch-thick glasses. Reto joined the Army, specifically the medical field, because he wants to be a doctor and have the Army pay for his schooling.

"Well, this is it. This is what we're here for." I try to calm him down and place my hand on his shoulder. Reto looks at me; his eyes are glossy and red.

"Thanks, man," he says quietly.

Reto and I hold eye contact for a second, letting each other know we're ready to do this, and together we head toward the OR. That's how it's always been with Reto and me. Even though we've only been friends for a few months, we have the silent communication down that usually takes friends years to master. It was easy for us because we are very similar and we remind each other of friends back home. Reto reminds me of my friend Sam, who wears glasses and is a hillbilly. Reto says I remind him of his friend Tom, who is tall and pale.

The main reason Reto and I click, is not because of our strong bond with each other but because of our lack of bonds with everyone else. If I had heard one of Denti's stupid stories in the real world I would have walked away. Same goes for almost everyone else. But Reto is my best friend because I know that after this year is over he's the only one I'll be talking to.

The OR is small. The smallest I've ever seen. In fact, every room in our hospital is small. We have everything a hospital must have—in miniature form. We have an OR (operating room), an ER (emergency room), an ICU (intensive care unit), an ICW (intensive care ward), a respiratory clinic, a mental health clinic, a patient administration section, an X-ray section, and a pharmacy. Everything you think a hospital should have—with the exception of a maternity ward.

In the OR we only do three surgeries at a time because that's the number of beds we have. Even worse is that in one of our rooms we have two OR beds placed only a few feet apart. This means we'll often have two surgeries going on at the same time in the same room. Not the most sterile setup in the world, but we're short on staff and short on space, just not short on patients.

The ICU and ICW can only hold sixteen patients each. This means a constant rotation going in and out. Whether the patients are Iraqi or American, we have to move them to another place as quickly as possible or we'll have no room for the incoming.

Reto and I grab our instrument trays and place them on the back table in the OR; this is where we'll work from during surgery. The room has just been mopped. The air is hot and smells of peroxide. I feel as though I am trapped in a bleach steam room. We walk around and check all our instruments to make sure they work. First is the bovie machine. It's a blue box that we use to cauterize the skin. Check. Next are the lights and the table. Check. Check. Last is the suction. It's bulky and looks like it's from the 1970s, but it works. Check.

Reto and I are doing our surgeries in the two-bed OR; we'll be right next to each other during surgery. Everything is set up, so it's time to gown and scrub in. The others still haven't shown up. A tall soldier walks over and tells us that since it's our first surgeries, members of the forward surgical team (FST) will shadow us. A forward surgical team is a small hospital unit trained to drop anywhere in the world and start a hospital within the hour. They have a reputation for being a bunch of cocky bastards.

I feel like puking I'm so nervous. I can feel my heart beating faster. I want to say I'm sick and back out. I wish that I'd chosen another job when I joined up—ER or ICU or ICW—anything but surgery. I wish I wasn't so impulsive and greedy. When I first thought about joining the military I took the ASVAB test (armed services vocational aptitude battery test). I got a great score, and the Army told me I could have practically any job I wanted. I told the recruiter that I'd take whichever job had the highest bonus and the biggest kicker for school. He said an OR medic gets an eight thousand dollar bonus and a monthly GI bill kicker (for college) of three hundred and fifty dollars. He did explain what an OR medic actually does, but at the age of seventeen I was too busy daydreaming about all of the magical things I could do with eight thousand dollars. Now here I am, three years later, and I would give back every cent to not be where I am. I would pay double, triple even, but I have no choice. The money is gone, the contract signed, and I am here in Iraq preparing for surgery.

0800 HOURS, OR

"You amateurs! Man, they don't teach you guys anything in school nowadays, do they?" I think this guy is Puerto Rican, but his voice gives no hint of an accent. He's this bowlegged FST soldier that comes barreling into the room. His face is covered with a mask for sterility purposes, but I can see his eyes as he talks.

"I can't believe you got all gowned and gloved and they don't tell you what has to happen."

Great. I haven't even started surgery and already this guy is berating me.

"Who's Specialist Anthony?" He asks, placing his hand in his pocket.

I raise my hand.

"I'm going to be shadowing you today. If we're going to be working together, you've got to learn how to do business. There is one way, and one way only! that we start off surgery, and I don't want you to forget that."

I nod.

The guy with bowlegs starts plugging in electronics while he's talking. "Rule one," he's intoning. "For What It's Worth" by Buffalo Springfield suddenly blares in the background. He quickly turns it down. "Get yourself an iPod." He's got the bass tuned exactly right now. "The last thing you want is to be stuck doing surgery for eight hours listening to some doctor talk about golf or politics."

0830 HOURS, SURGERY

"What's your name, soldier?" asks the doctor I'll be working with. He's in his late fifties or early sixties. He's skinny, skinnier than I am, and slightly smaller, around 5'7". He stands with a slouch, though, and if he stood up straight we might be the same height.

"Specialist Anthony." I begin to gown and glove the doctor.

"I am Colonel Jessop," he says as the nurses wheel our patients in the room and place them on the OR tables. "There are only a few things I ask of you. Just do whatever I tell you to do. Learn quickly and give me what I need before I need it. Do all these things and we'll get along just fine. And call me Bill."

That's how it's always been in the OR. Even though we're in the military and Bill is a colonel, we keep it casual. When you're doing surgery and you've got a person bleeding to death you don't have time to say, "Colonel Jessop, sir, the patient is bleeding. What should I do?" You yell, "Bill, we've got a bleeder. Get down here now!" That's the one perk of the OR—the doctors and anesthesiologists, who are colonels and majors, take off all rank and relax once in the OR. It's not about who has the higher position, it's about working together as peers and getting the job done. This in itself helps ease the anxiety—somewhat. But a patient's life is still in my hands, in our hands.

My job is simple enough. Just like Bill said, all I need to do is what I'm told and whenever possible before I'm told. Basically, it's like in the movies. A doctor yells out "Scalpel!" and then a gloved hand reaches over and gives it to him. That hand is an OR medic's hand—my hand.

I fall automatically into surgery mode. Life or death doesn't matter to me right now. My only concern is to do my job the best I can. We're taught in operating room technician school that it's the family's job to worry; our job is to save lives. When I first had someone say that to me, I was skeptical. I thought it was just a cute saying that people in the medical field would say to one another. Then during training I had my first surgery. It was on a woman, and I was so worried about screwing up and having the patient die that I handed the doctor the wrong instruments. The patient still survived, though. When I got out of surgery, I saw her family waiting, and I felt so happy to see their relief when they heard their mother/wife had made it through the surgery. But I also felt shame because I hadn't given my best in there. I spent too much time worrying and messed up.

Before I know it, everything fades into oblivion. I can no longer hear the music. I can no longer hear Reto's surgery only a few feet away. I can no longer hear all the beeps and buzzes from the machines. All I can hear is the voice of my surgeon as he yells: "Scalpel!" "Bovie!" "Suction!" "Suture!"

Eventually even Bill's voice fades away. We form a flow. I am inside his head. Our surgery is an I&D (irrigation and debridement) on an Iraqi civilian injured by a suicide bomber. Bill performed exploratory surgery on him yesterday and plugged all his holes. Now we are irrigating the wound to keep it clean and removing all the shrapnel we can find so the patient doesn't get an infection. In this case, the shrapnel is human bone from the suicide bomber. When the bomber blew himself up, chunks of his bones went flying everywhere, and now they are embedded in our patient. The surgery is like any other, but the fact that we're removing human bone makes it harder. For most bomb explosions, metal is embedded in the victims and it is easily findable with an X-ray. However, with human bone, when an X-ray is done, if the shrapnel hit in a certain part, sometimes it's not possible to distinguish between the patient's bone and someone else's bone fragments.

Everyone is too close in this room! Even under all of our sterile protective wear I can feel everyone's breath on me. It makes me anxious. I didn't go through all my training to become certified only to come here and have people watch my every move. I haven't screwed up yet, but all this attention is making me think too much, and thinking is when I get myself into trouble. I need to stop thinking; I just need to do. That's what I always tell myself since that first surgery with the woman. I don't care if the patient dies, it's only about if I do my job well. That doctor told me I was one of the best technicians he ever had. When I saw the patient's family and how happy they were, though, I felt nothing. No happiness, no shame, no pride, nothing—my job isn't to feel.

"Hand the doctor the final suture," the guy with bowlegs—Specialist Trask—tells me. I've only known him for an hour and already I can't stand him. His voice makes the hairs on the back of my neck stand up. He's so close to me that I can smell his deodorant, Old Spice Original Style. I long for the civilian world OR, where you've got room to move around and no one is looking over your shoulder.

I hand the doctor the suture and he begins closing the wound. The surgery is almost over. I look down and there's hardly any blood.

"Nice work, Anthony." Bill looks up at me. "You don't need the FST guy hanging around you."

I nod my head. "Thank you, Colonel. . . ."

"Soldier," Bill says cutting me off. "I respect your bearing, but remember we're in the OR, it's Bill."

"All right."

"You got an iPod?"

"Yes, Bill."

"Trask has the worst taste in music."

He starts taking his gown off.

"Next time you see my name on the surgery board, sign up to work with me and bring Classical."

Trask is closing up the wound.

Bill is looking at his watch.

I am also grateful for having met Dr. Bill—actually, he's given me hope. For a while there I was starting to think that I would never meet someone I could look up to and respect, that maybe my standards were too high, that maybe Gagney, the staff sergeant in charge of the operating room (OR) section where I work, is as good as it gets.

Gagney: late thirties. His eyes are brown, his hair is black, and on the crown of his head is a bald spot. He looks to be a mixture of Native American, Portuguese, and Italian. He claims to be none of the above and will not tell me his ethnicity. Back during our three-and-a-half-month pre-deployment training in Wisconsin, he received divorce papers from his wife and then spent twenty minutes calling Reto and me idiots because we didn't have pens on us. Then a month ago Gagney, Reto, Denti, and I were playing Risk, a game of global domination. I had an alliance with Reto and we attacked Gagney's armies. Gagney flipped out, knocked the game board over, called us all "fucking idiot cheaters," and stormed off. I've seen him yell at a female soldier while she sobbed uncontrollably.

This is the guy who's supposed to be, I mean *is*, our leader in Iraq.

1100 HOURS, OR

"Look who decides to show up," Reto says.

Almost our entire OR team is on their way in. Sergeants and specialists like shift leader Hudge—Mexican, she's as pale as I am, attractive, twenty-four years old, and married to another specialist working as a medic in our unit's ER. I know she's a strong woman who isn't afraid to speak her mind, but most importantly I know that she is very emotional. In the past few months, every time I've seen her, she has either been yelling or crying.

What a beginning. Almost everybody is late, including Gagney, and it's only our first day at work.

For some reason Gagney thinks now is a good time to assert his authority as the alpha male of our group.

"Come here, sergeant!" yells Gagney to Elster, a Dominican sergeant.

"Yes, sir," Elster says as he quickly approaches.

Gagney continues yelling, his voice is hard and stern like an angered father.

"You're late! This is a hospital! This is the military! You show up late and someone dies!"

Gagney is directing his tirade at Elster, but he looks over at all of us to see if we're watching.

"Your tardiness could have cost someone their life!"

Gagney starts to get into character now. His arms are flailing, fingers pointing at Elster. "Do you understand? You're staying late tonight!"

Gagney then turns and speaks to all of us. "Go have lunch! Because starting at 1300, we're dealing with a mock mass casualty situation."

I don't know whether to clap at Gagney's performance or worry that it's just the beginning of a long year. I feel bad for Elster. During training in Wisconsin he got made fun of for having an effeminate voice and for listening to Michael Bolton. He also likes the Beatles; he's the whitest black guy I know.

But watching Gagney yell at him for no reason twists my stomach in a knot. It's one thing for me to get yelled at, at least I've mastered the art of daydreaming, but watching someone else being yelled at is like watching a car crash. You feel bad and can't take your eyes off of it, but there's nothing you can do, so you keep on driving and say a little prayer.

We all go to lunch—except for Elster.

1230 HOURS, OR

A mass casualty is a surge of patients coming in all at once, possibly more than we can handle. For the mock scenario, soldiers from around the base come in and pretend to be wounded. We have to act out what we'd do if the injuries were real. It usually goes something like this: The fake patients come into the ER. The doctors and medics look them over and say what is wrong with them and where they need to go depending on their injuries. The ones with small or manageable wounds are sent to the ICU or ICW, and the ones who need surgery are sent to the OR.

During a mass casualty, however, there are also patients you send off to die. With our limited capabilities, doctors need to make tough decisions. Eight patients come in for surgery, but you can only do three at a time. That means five lie back and wait. If the wounds are bad enough, then there's nothing we can do for them, except call a chaplain to read them their last rites.

"So you're telling me that all we can do is watch patients die?" Reto asks as we sit and wait for the fake patients.

"Depending on their wounds, yeah," I say. "Some of them."

Dr. Bill jumps in. "Say we have eight patients and three need twelve hours of surgery, but only five need three hours of surgery. Those five could die while we spent twelve hours on the other three patients. Even though we can and know how to save everyone's life, we can't."

I hear Gagney yelling at Sergeant Hudge in another room. He's been like this all day, pacing back and forth yelling at people: *Do this. Do that. Stop that.*

"In fact, for the real bad patients," Dr. Bill is continuing, "it would be better for them if we just left them to die in the field. At least there they would have a quick death. All we do by bringing them back here is prolong the inevitable. It's horrible."

Staff Sergeant Gagney comes out of the room and sees us talking to Dr. Bill.

"What are you doing just sitting down?"

I look at Gagney. "We've got eight patients on the way." The ER hasn't sent us any fake patients back yet.

"Get your rooms ready." Gagney is acting as if we've got twenty on the way.

"The rooms are set up," I say.

"Listen, soldier." Gagney talks over me at a volume higher than necessary. "ER might have two patients with gunshot wounds coming over. I want you gowned and gloved and sitting in that OR waiting for those patients to come in."

I was about to stand up, to show him respect, but I change my mind.

"This is a test," he says.

"If it were a real mass casualty, we wouldn't do that," I'm saying. "If this is supposed to be real, then we'd sit out here and wait."

"Stand up when you talk to a superior officer."

I shouldn't be saying this. "It could be an hour—"

"I don't care if you wait for ten hours. I want you in there now." Gagney stares at me.

I stand up reluctantly. It's all I can think to do. I look around the room. Everyone's watching, but no one says anything. I look at the others. I see the sympathy in their eyes, but no words of encouragement are forthcoming. Everyone is afraid of Gagney's temper—and no one wants to be on the wrong end of it.

Gagney continues to yell. "It goes for the rest of you, too," Gagney booms. "I don't care how long it takes. I don't care how hot it is in there. Gown up and go into your rooms and stay there." Everyone gets up.

"I don't care if you have to go to the bathroom. No one leaves until I tell you you can go!"

I stare at Gagney and recall a thought I've had many times in the Army. I cut my hair at least every twelve days, and I wear the same uniform without fail because I signed a contract three years ago. The contract says that all my decisions are to be made by somebody else who is my superior. He is my shepherd and I must follow. I am nothing more than a sheep being led into a dry, desolate desert. I must follow my shepherd if I want to get out alive—or at least that's what I'm told.

1600 HOURS, BREAK ROOM

"Let's cut the guy some slack," says Sellers, the only one to come to Gagney's defense. As if his performance at the mock mass casualty wasn't salt enough in the wound, he then puts Hudge and Chandler on second shift, which started at 1500 hours. (Chandler is a twenty-eight-year-old mechanic from the backwoods of Maine. He's even more "country" than Reto—and missing more teeth than he has.)

Gagney placed Waters and Sellers on third shift. Everyone else needs to be back tomorrow morning at 0700 while Gagney gets to stroll in whenever he wants because he's still working on a final schedule.

Maybe she's right; maybe we are being too harsh on him. I nod in agreement with Sellers. She looks at me as if trying to find out if she can trust me or not. She's not sure she can trust anyone, ever since someone started a rumor about her being a lesbian a couple of weeks ago. She denied it—then got caught fooling around with a girl during our stopover in Kuwait. She refuted it again and accused her detractors of conducting a witch-hunt against her. However the rumor—and her mistrust—persist.

Reto blurts out from his chair: "I don't care if it's day one or one hundred. That guy is an asshole."

Denti says he doesn't want to waste any more time on the douchebag and gets up to leave the break room. I don't say it, but I think Sellers is right. Just do your job. Give it a few weeks. There's a lot to get used to for everybody. Maybe military life hasn't been all I thought it would be. I pictured men and women shoulders back and heads held high, living their lives by virtuous ideals and proud to wear the uniform of their country—maybe I'm not that naïve. I saw a military marching, flying the American flag, singing the national anthem, and defeating all our enemies without losing a single man. But I think there's something behind that, that in the end it's right and it works, and we can trust that—we have to be able to trust that.

1900 HOURS, GYM

Bunkers are cement shelters designed for mortar attacks. They run about four feet high and around fifteen feet long. There's room enough for about twenty people. The first thing we're told to do when we enter a new building is locate the closest bunkers.

In Iraq we carry our M-16s with us everywhere we go, and that includes the shower, the dining facility, and the gym. When I first started carrying the weapon around, it felt awkward having to take it with me everywhere. I even had to balance it on the bathroom floor while I relieved myself. Now, after all these months of having to carry it around everyday, it still feels unnatural and cumbersome. Back home, my friends talk in awe about what it's like to be a soldier and a man, someone who walks around all day with a weapon, but I don't tell any of them the truth. The truth is that I don't feel like a real man. A real man would have a choice in the matter, but in my case it is merely an order. In the end, though, I know it's for my own good to carry the weapon with me everywhere. I'm learning weapon awareness, and if I ever come upon an enemy soldier, I will have my weapon ready to fire and kill.

Although sometimes I can't stand Denti and the stories he tells—like the time he told me he had a girl pee on him, or how he had sex with an Asian prostitute—it's pretty cool being at the gym with him. Since he is allegedly a former powerlifter—not that he isn't a great bullshitter at all times—he says he'll get me jacked by the time I go back home. I figure I don't have much else planned while in Iraq, so I might as well go to the gym when I can.

Denti's workout is very thorough: sit-ups, push-ups, leg work, benching. Most of the time he's screaming at me—either telling me I'm doing something wrong or yelling in some type of weird powerlifting congratulatory manner when I do something right.

I'm spotting Denti and Reto comes over, finished with cardio.

Then we hear the sound of this car door slamming: *Bang. Bang. Bang.*

The runners stop running and look at the weightlifters to see if the noise was the weights banging. The weightlifters stop lifting and look at the people playing basketball to see if the noise was a ball bouncing. Everyone turns and looks at the cyclers, who have stopped riding.

Loud noises. *Boom. Boom. Boom.* Louder than I've ever heard before, like fireworks and thunder all together.

Freeze.

Suddenly everyone's rushing toward the weapons rack, grabbing guns, running outside.

The explosions are coming closer now, closer together, one on top of the other.

We're sprinting for the bunkers. I'm breathing deep, it's twenty-five feet away. Crouching down as I enter.

Huge crash, very close.

"Get the fuck in there now!" Denti yells.

Bbbbbooooommmmmm.

It's hitting the dome right outside. Mortar, a huge bullet fired from a cannon explodes and sends shrapnel flying over and into people. A second later and Denti could have died. I look at Denti and try to gauge how he's feeling since he came the closest to getting hit. It's too dark to see Denti's face, though. More mortars are going off and hitting around the gym. Since it's a huge dome, it's an easy enough target. We look around; there are fifteen people in the bunker. It's pitch-dark; I can't see who is with us in the bunker. I sit there and replay what just happened. I'm not sure how I'm supposed to feel about the whole thing. I've never had a near-death experience before, and I'm not sure how to react. Everyone else is just sitting in silence. I feel like I should be happy to be alive; I feel like I should have a newfound perspective on life, but I don't know what I feel. It's no emotion I've ever heard described before. I can't describe it with a word like *nervous*, *scared*, or *afraid*; I've felt all those before, but never before have I felt the feeling of almost dying.

"Who grabbed my ass?" a burly male voice yells out. Everyone in the bunker laughs. No one seems fazed by the attack and how close Denti came to injury or death.

"I grabbed it and I'd do it again," a different male voice yells out. This brings even more laughter. I try to force myself to laugh with all of them, but I am still shaken up. I almost died and people are making jokes. Intellectually, I know that joking about a situation should help, but I don't feel like joking. I'm just not there yet.

The mortar rounds continue to go off, some sounding on the other side of the base and some hitting next to us. Everyone goes on talking and laughing as if we aren't in danger, as if this is no big deal, as if people almost die all the time. Denti lights up a cigarette. I'm riled up so Denti offers me one. I normally don't smoke, but I take a cigarette anyway. As I take my first puff, I start to relax.

The lights from the cigarettes illuminate the inside of the bunker and we can finally see the hints of each other's faces. Everyone looks relaxed and calm. My heart is still racing, but I begin to realize that I will have to learn to accept that the base being mortared and me jumping into a bunker is going to be a part of my life for the next year. I can either sit and wallow in fear or learn to laugh like the rest of them.

1915 HOURS, BUNKERS

Fifteen minutes go by. No further rounds go off. A soldier gets a call on his radio saying it's all clear, we're safe to walk around again. Emerging, we're looking at the damage to the bunkers. Amazingly, there hasn't been any structural damage, the concrete was so thick. The gym is alright, too. The ground surrounding, however, is a different story. Although there's only a small indentation in the ground where the mortar hit, the area is covered in bits and pieces of metal—shrapnel. Someone picks up a piece, it's hot; it burns his hand.

We decide to start walking. Our hospital policy dictates that everyone must report in after a mortar attack to count who's still alive, and we don't have radios.

"You know I almost got hit by that," Denti brags. "I jumped into the bunker at the last second."

People seem impressed and Denti is proud. I look at Denti and laugh. I'm happy that his near-death experience hasn't scarred him for life, but I know I will have to hear the retelling of this story, again and again.

1930 HOURS, BASE ROAD

As we start our trek back to the hospital, I notice that it's dark and the base has a new feel to it. This is our home—but we are not safe here. I think this is what the enemy is trying to accomplish: They want us on alert until it burns us out. The worst part is thinking about how it could happen at any time or at any place. It makes me feel like a prisoner inside a prison that I was sent to liberate. I think I can finally realize a name for my feeling. It's the feeling of impending doom. I could be dead or mortally wounded anywhere, at any time.

The moon, standing alone in the sky, is our only light. My legs are tired from the workout at the gym; it feels like we have been walking forever. We pass the dining facility and the Iraqi-run Hajji stores that sell bootleg DVDs and cigarettes. We aren't seeing damage from mortars; the rest must have hit on the other side of the base.

It becomes hypnotic, the noise of each step we take; they're the only distinguishable sounds within earshot. None of us speak as we walk. This must be what the world would feel like after a nuclear war.

"We're the only people on the street," says Reto. He and Denti light cigarettes and I stop and look around. We're standing in-between streetlights and there's a fence on either side of us. Up ahead are buildings. This is the busiest street on the base and there is no sound, only Denti throwing his old cigarette to the ground. It feels like impending doom, like something's going to happen, like people felt on New Year's Eve 1999, at 11:59 and 58 seconds, possibly the end of the world.

"Where the hell is everyone? If it's all clear, where are they?" Reto asks.

I think for a second. "They're probably all at their units checking in."

I have a cigarette with them, even though I don't smoke. It's my second in the country, a pretty worthwhile occasion I would say—just nearly got my head blown off. The nicotine kicks in fast and is relaxing. We see a Humvee speeding down the road behind us. It pulls up next to us, but the window doesn't roll down.

"What the hell's going on?" Reto asks.

I'm really starting to get nervous: "Fuck, man. . . ."

The window cracks open: "What are you guys doing walking around? It hasn't been all cleared yet; get to some fucking bunkers now!"

And then it leaves, speeding away. Reto's hand shakes as he puts the cigarette to his mouth and grips his weapon.

Denti's head jerks back and forth as he looks in all directions. "Do you guys see any bunkers anywhere?"

We start running, running as fast as we can for the hospital. I've never run this fast before, none of us have, and probably never will. When we reach that front door at the hospital I look down; my hands are shaking, too. As we head inside the main lobby we hear a loud explosion, followed by an even louder one.

After a while, staff for our unit check in one by one to let everyone know that they're alive. Some are scared; some excited. It's strange to see the ones excited about a mortar attack.

Someone from another part of the hospital comes in and tells us we shouldn't be here. We should have stayed in the bunker. Nothing's all clear until there's an announcement on the loudspeaker.

A soldier pokes his head through a door and yells into our room. "Don't send anyone home. We've got a mass casualty. This is real."

My anxiety from this morning returns. Inside I'm screaming. I want to throw up, it's too much fucking pressure, I can't take it, I can't fucking hack it. I wish I had gone to college. If I had gone to college I would only be worried about girls and midterms, but instead I am worrying whether or not I can save someone's life, and whether or not all my worrying could cost them their life.

We hear shouting and a lot of commotion coming from the ER. The first casualties are arriving: two Iraqis and an American soldier; the American soldier is from the unit we're replacing. He was hit by shrapnel in the second attack. He was going home in a few days. A year in Iraq he survives everything, then a week before he's supposed to leave he gets injured.

The medics and doctors in the ER are looking the patients over, deciding what type of care they need.

The same soldier who told us not to leave sticks his head through the door. He tells us two Iraqis need surgery. A gunshot wound to the leg and arm. The other has shrapnel to the head and neck.

We've got to ready our instruments. Before we can grab our instrument trays, the ER soldier is back: "Four injured Iraqis on the way. All need surgery. Not sure about wounds, sounds like all GSWs [gunshot wounds]."

Six patients now need surgery—three OR beds. Grab Basic Instrument sets: different clamps, scissors, retractors, and forceps. Don't fucking think!

I'm in the single room. Denti is in the double room with Torres—a thirty-one-year-old with broken English from Guatemala. Torres joined the Army, specifically the medical field, because his younger brother joined the Army and died while in combat—in Iraq.

Prepare for an all-nighter. "Four more on the way, they're thirty minutes out." The Soldier yells again, for the third and hopefully final time.

2100 HOURS, OR

It's complete chaos. The FST people try to take over operations of the hospital. Gagney's all pissed off and he starts yelling again. Not only is he getting in everyone's way, he's annoying the doctors.

The three surgeries are going quickly. I'm working on an Iraqi that needs both his arm and leg amputated. The injured American isn't as bad as they thought; he can wait to be seen until tomorrow. Torres and Denti are working on Iraqi patients.

Working on the Iraqi relaxes me a little bit. I know I'm doing my best to try to save him, but I also know that, truthfully, if he dies it won't be as big a deal as if an American dies. If that happened on my table, everyone would read about it back in the States and his name would be on a wall, forever engraving my inability not to save his life. But if an Iraqi dies, I know that most likely he will be given a pauper's funeral, and back in the States his name won't appear except as a statistic. It's not a pleasant thing to think about, but I need something to take the edge off.

Everything moves like a dream. It's finally here. It feels more intense than I ever imagined. Everyone is doing exactly what they did this afternoon. I can feel myself slowly put a wall up, though. I'm unconsciously separating myself from any emotion that might be bubbling to the surface. I look around at everyone in the OR with me: the doctor, the nurse, the anesthesiologist. It seems like everyone else is on autopilot, too. Today is just another day in a place nobody will ever hear of. I look at some of the doctors and they are laughing, full of energy and ready to work all night if need be. I can tell they've perfected the emotion block. I'm trained for it too, even if I need to get better at it in the operating room, and out.

2300 HOURS, OR

I overhear a conversation between Dr. Bill and Gagney in the next room.

"Listen, you may be in charge of the OR for the enlisted section, but I am in charge of the ENTIRE OR. No one needs to hear you losing your shit. You aren't helping anyone by screaming your head off. In fact, you're hurting the situation. I let it go this afternoon because it was only a mock scenario. But right now, this is happening. People are injured and could die. You're going to cause more damage; you have to relax. Come back tomorrow, leave, get a level head."

Gagney is visibly embarrassed and I see him lower his eyes to the ground. I avoid eye contact as he walks past me.

0100 HOURS, OR

There are just a few of us left. Sellers is out back working diligently putting together instrument trays; Waters chatters on about nothing.

Back home in the States, she's a waitress at a strip club, but I have a feeling every woman who works there says they're a "waitress." Waters continues speaking, and the more she does, the more I can tell we are never going to get along. She has the undeserving self-worth of a high school prom queen who now works at a strip club, and I have the deserving self-worth of a wallflower that never went to his prom. I know that she is the type of girl who will use her sex appeal to get her way, and I know that I am the type of guy to fall for it. "Hey girls," I say, with Reto standing next to me. "Are you all good? It's late and we've got to be back for an eight hour shift in a few hours."

I've seen the look Waters then gives me many times before. It's the look I get while talking to a girl that thinks she's out of my league.

"Gagney did screw us over the most." She bats her eyelashes. "Maybe you can stay a little later. Besides, you guys need the practice. So you two should stay and do the next cases."

Waters turns soft then as she changes tactics and tries to convince us of the virtues of staying late. "Gagney will probably let you come in late anyway. You're young too, and don't need much sleep. Besides, I'm sure there will be plenty of late nights. You might as well get used to it."

We should have just fucking told them we were leaving instead of asking. Reto has now fallen for her trap and decides to take one of the cases. Waters takes the other one. I stay for another hour and help put instrument sets back together. As I leave for the night, their patients are just coming in. I tell Reto I'll cover for him so he can sleep late tomorrow.

0200 HOURS, MY ROOM

When I get back to my room, my new roommate is asleep and snoring. Reto told me his name is Specialist Markham. He sounds like a hibernating bear with sleep apnea. He's probably going to die, but I'm too tired to care.

Do I wake up in four hours at 0600 to eat then go to work, or do I wake up in four and a half hours at 0630, skip breakfast, and go directly to work? I'm asleep before I can even think about it.

WEEK 1, DAY 3, IRAQ

0600 HOURS, BARRACKS

My eyes crack open at the sound of my alarm. I only went to sleep four hours ago, and now I have another full day ahead of me. Markham is still asleep and snoring. I want to "accidentally" make some noise as I get dressed because my pounding headache is being aggravated by the sound of him choking on his tongue. I slam my door as I leave to go to Denti's room.

Denti is wide-awake, smiling, well rested; he went back to his room after the first case. He's lighting up a cigarette, telling me I look like shit. I have to stop myself from hitting him, all hair-gelled and teeth brushed. He's so full of bullshit.

"Hey man, remember yesterday at the gym when I almost died?" We're walking along the road to the dining facility on the same road the Humvee stopped us. A crowd of people is standing around and taking pictures.

There's a six-inch-deep and two-foot-wide indentation in the ground. In the parking lot, Humvees are peppered with shrapnel; all their front tires are blown out, and the tires on one of them have melted into the ground.

A soldier taking a picture says, "It happened last night during the second attack."

"Holy shit!" Denti gasps.

"We were standing in this exact spot last night. Two times in one day I was almost . . ." Denti begins and trails off. No one is listening. No one cares how close he, Reto, and I almost came to dying. Three more people in the crowd speak up about their own near-death experiences last night. Millions of people almost die every day, and thousands do die everyday. But listen, I don't have to be psychic to guess what Denti's thinking; I know how his mind works . . . *These people on the road may not be impressed, but they're gonna love it in the D-fac at breakfast.*

"So there I was . . ." "Minutes away . . ." "No I wasn't scared . . ." "The bomb hit right after we'd . . . ," "Seriously, I was minutes away from death."

I'm just shoveling it in.

0700 HOURS, OR

When we get to work we have four cases already lined up. They are all I&Ds for the mass casualty patients from yesterday. As we prepare, Specialist Torres and Reto come in.

Denti and I have our rooms set up for surgery, but no one is here yet. We take our gowns and gloves off and head to the break room to wait for the doctors. They're most likely tired from last night, too, but unlike us, they can come to work whenever they want.

Torres, Reto, and I complain about having to wait around for the doctors, but we shouldn't. It's an unexpected break and we don't see too many of those.

0800 HOURS, OR

Staff Sergeant Gagney walks in; he is an hour late for work and Reto and I stare at him as he saunters into the room and plops himself in a chair near us.

"Aargh," Gagney sighs, trying to make a production of how tired he is.

"Man, am I tired. Hey Reto, go make me a cup of coffee, will you?" Gagney says as he pushes further back in his chair.

"I was up late all night working on a schedule for you guys," he says, as he gives a fake yawn.

Reto just stares at Gagney with fire in his eyes and doesn't move to get him a cup of coffee. I try to avoid eye contact with Gagney so he won't ask me to go.

"Aaaghh," Gagney sighs again as he now stands from his chair, feeling satisfied that we understand how hard he worked and why he has an excuse for being late. He walks over to the break room and posts the schedule on the door. It's three pages of yellow-lined paper and only covers this month.

As Reto, Torres, and I are crowding around the door to read the schedule, Denti walks over and rips the schedule from the door: "For Christ sake. Look at the schedule. Anthony. You're on first shift today; tomorrow you're on second shift. The day after that you're on third shift and the day after that first shift."

He starts talking to me slowly as if I'm a child. "That means tomorrow you work three to eleven. But the next day, you work eleven to seven, got me? And the day after that you work seven to three. That means you'll be working sixteen hours."

Reto grabs the schedule and starts analyzing it.

"How the hell are we going to sleep if our shifts change every day? Elster, Gagney, Hudge, and Waters all have the same shifts every day. It's just us fucking specialists getting screwed over."

Torres grabs the schedule from Reto. I know he can barely understand it, but he stares at it as if he is reading a book. "So what does this mean? We will be working a different shift every other day? Why? That doesn't make sense."

"It means we're getting screwed. Gagney is such an idiot!"

0900 HOURS, OR

"Needle holder . . ." Dr. Bill yells, taking me out of my daze. I don't know how many times he's asked for it, but I grab the closest one and hand it to him. It's the wrong kind, but he uses it.

1445 HOURS, OR

When I first met Chandler at our training in Wisconsin, I didn't like him. He seemed too goofy for me to be able to talk to or take seriously, but as the days go on and we've formed a common enemy—no, not Al Qaeda or Osama bin Laden, Staff Sergeant Gagney—I would say we're now friends. In fact, the first day I met him, he had a saying that summed up how people feel about him: "I'm like mold. You may not like me at first, but I grow on you." He had all kinds of bumper sticker sayings like that. He once even told me a line that he wrote in a Valentine to his fiancée, Jill: "My love for you is like herpes. It may subside at times, but it will never leave you."

Denti is ripping the schedule off the door again. "He has us changing shifts every other fucking day." Hudge and Chandler are looking at it now.

"What!" Chandler squeaks out as he spits up the sip of Pepsi he was drinking.

That's another thing about Chandler. It seems like he has a can of Pepsi permanently glued to his hand.

"You have got to be fucking kidding me," Denti is going on. "First of all, there are no days off scheduled for any of us, except for Gagney. Next to his name in parentheses it says, 'will make own days off,' whatever that means."

"This is wicked retarded," Hudge says, her voice thick with a Boston accent.

Chandler starts laughing.

"Look at this. Gagney and Elster are on first shift every day together. I'm sure that's going to be fun," Denti says, making reference to our first day where Gagney chewed him out in front of all of us.

"It always seems to be something with this guy doesn't it?" Hudge says. "He can't even make a schedule without somehow making it the worst schedule possible."

"We've got to say something," Chandler says. "We can't let this stand. He's probably just trying to make a point that he can do whatever he wants. You want to know what the worst part is, and no offense Hudge, but the reason that Elster, Waters, and you are all on shifts that don't change is because Gagney knows you three are the most vocal people. He knows that the rest of us probably won't complain."

"Fuck that, I'll walk right up to him and shove the schedule down his throat," Denti angrily exclaims.

Reto jumps from his chair. "Let's go talk to him."

The six of us walk together toward the main OR, we're like a gang about to kick some ass. I start snapping my fingers and bobbing my shoulders like in *West Side Story*.

"We need to talk about the schedule," Hudge announces as we reach Gagney's desk.

He is busy playing a computer game and doesn't look up.

"What is it!" he says as he starts to shut down his computer.

"Well," Hudge says, her confidence starting to subside, "We just had a few concerns about the schedule we wanted to talk about."

Gagney's computer is now off, but he still hasn't turned around to look at any of us. He stands and grabs his weapon and his jacket from the back of his chair.

"Well, there shouldn't be a problem. Like I said, it's not permanent. I still have to work guard duty into it."

"There seems to be—" Hudge is saying.

"But this is the military, so I suggest you find a way to deal with whatever problems you have. The schedule sticks so deal with it." Gagney doesn't make eye contact with any of us as he walks out the door.

We are all left standing there. Denti, who said he would shove the schedule down Gagney's throat, looks like he's about to cry. His voice is trembling and he sounds like a child.

"Fucking unbelievable."

Hudge is especially silent. Right now she isn't one of us. After all, she has the comfort of working the same time every day while our schedules are changing.

"Maybe he just doesn't understand what's wrong with the schedule. Maybe if we explain things to him . . ." says Chandler. He already knows his plan isn't going to work.

"Listen guys, go back to your rooms and get some sleep or go eat. I'll try to talk to Gagney when I can. Maybe even Dr. Bill can help." Hudge's voice is now calm and caring; she sounds more like a mother than a soldier. We feel some comfort knowing that she has this side to her. That even with everything that's going on we still can have someone who truly cares about us . . . even if they . . . aren't going to do anything.

1600 HOURS, OR

My quick notes on three women:

Hudge met her husband in the military. She loves chocolate. If she starts craving chocolate she'll do almost anything for it, even give you a back rub.

I'm still not sure if Sellers is a lesbian. I flirt with her and she flirts back, but after work she spends time with the other lesbians in our unit. I spend a lot of time with Sellers because she is an insomniac and she'll come in on every shift. Most of the time she does more work than the person on shift. She is also a major germophobe; she washes her hands once before going to the bathroom and twice after. She puts gloves on to floss her teeth, and she uses an entire roll of toilet paper whenever she goes to the bathroom—and that's just to build a nest on the toilet seat.

I also met another officer I'll be working with. Captain Tarr is a Caucasian woman from Washington State. Although she often tries to tell people she is in her forties, the crows-feet around her eyes and mouth give her away. She looks good for a woman in her fifties, though, and you can tell that she used to be attractive when she was younger. She's married, has two kids, and gives a killer back rub. Often I'll be sitting there and she'll come up behind me and start rubbing away—these are on her good days. She does have bad days, too. Or I guess it's more good hours and bad hours. One minute she'll be giving you a back rub and the next she'll be cursing at you for unplugging the coffee maker. I've learned to wait and see how she acts around other people before I approach her. I'm worried she is bipolar.

WEEK 3, DAY 1, IRAQ

2200 HOURS, MY ROOM

Beep. Beep. Beep.

It's ten at night, but it's morning to me. It is my second day in a row on third shift and I've got to be at work in one hour. I'm still tired and Markham is sleeping next to me. He always sleeps well and his schedule never changes. As a laboratory technician, he tests blood to make sure it's good to put in patients and collects it from donors when our supplies run low. I'm working eight hours, then I get eight hours off, then I'm back on for eight hours. Two days ago, I was on first shift. Gagney didn't come in to work; he gave himself a day off. It's been two weeks and none of us have had a day off. Gagney's had two.

0300 HOURS, OR

Waters wakes from her nap (inside the supply closet) and finds that I have fallen asleep while working on putting instrument trays together.

"Anthony, wake up! What are you doing sleeping on the job?"

I put my arms in the air and open my eyes as best as I can. "Whhatt?"

"You were late. I had to stand around waiting for you."

"I'm sorry, I fell back asleep, I told you—"

"I don't want to hear it, you were on this shift with me yesterday, two days in a row; your body should be on schedule."

I knew little about her. Besides being a "waitress," she's a registered nurse. She says she makes more money working at the strip club so she does that instead. I get an image of Waters in my head working at the strip club and having men slip dollar bills into her thong. If only they knew later on she'd be fighting for their freedom.

"Get the sterilizer machines ready. You didn't finish the work you were supposed to do; now we'll both have to do it." Waters starts rummaging around the room. I'm not sure what she's looking for.

"Didn't you do anything while I was sleeping?!" She screams.

I come out of my daze enough to realize that Waters is asking a rhetorical question. She doesn't want an answer but I decide to answer anyway. "I didn't do anything while you were sleeping! God forbid you should do anything, actually do some—I'm sooo sorry that Waters has to do work. God forbid, I fall asleep and you might actually—I'm switching shifts every other day. My sleeping and eating are all fucked up and you might actually have to do something—you might actually have to do something yourself like some of your own work. . . ."

I'm tired; I'm not thinking straight, I keep talking.

"You've been on third shift every day since we got here. Have you even done any surgeries since our first mass cal? Third shift never gets the surgeries. You sleep your entire fucking shift!" For the first time in two weeks I feel as though a burden has been lifted off of my chest, as if the yelling has released all of my pent-up anger. Waters breaks eye contact first; her eyes go to the floor and she starts working. I start working and we finish up what we had to do. After that we go to opposite sides of the OR. Waters starts reading a *People* magazine; I'm writing in my journal.

WEEK 3, DAY 6, IRAQ

0645 HOURS, MY ROOM

Beep. Beep. Beep. Beep. Beep. Beep. Beep. Beep.

"Turn that thing off," my roommate Markham says as he throws a pillow at me. I open my eyes and stare at him. I don't know what's going on—

"Wwwhhhatt . . . thheehhell . . ."

Markham shuts my alarm off.

"Gagney is really screwing you guys over. I didn't think you could get any whiter than you are, but you look like a fucking holocaust victim."

"What time is it?" I grumble as I start to get out of bed.

"Six forty six," Markham replies.

I need to be at work at 0700.

0705 HOURS, OR

Reto and Torres tell me that Gagney is taking a day off and that Elster is in charge of us. I can't remember the last time I smiled like this. The world seems like a better place. Captain Tarr approaches us and I smile at her.

"What do you think you're smiling at!?! You came in here late. You think you can come in late just because Gagney is taking a day off?"

I quickly snap to the position of attention. Even though she is not my boss, she is higher ranking so I have to show her the proper respect.

"This is incredible. You men are all the same. You think you can get away with anything. When the cat's away, the mouse will play."

Captain Tarr continues to ramble and I notice that she's starting to not make sense. She's been acting strange for a few days now—stranger than I've seen her before. Normally her mood is up and down; she's either giving you a massage or verbally strangling you, but now it's as if her mood is constantly on one side—the bad one. And I know I'm not the only one who's noticed it. Just yesterday Reto told me she yelled at him for using the last piece of paper in a notebook. The day before that she yelled at Denti and threw a pen at him because he ate the last muffin in the break room.

She continues to yell and I stare at the middle of her forehead. I refuse to give her the respect of my eye contact as she screams at me.

"Unbelievable . . . piece of . . . you should be . . . screw. . . ." She yells and yells and I can't help but wonder if there isn't some type of heavy suppressed anger underneath. Something must be eating her up, and she's taking it out on all of us. But she continues to yell, and I begin to wonder what it would be like if she and Gagney had a child. I wonder if it's really possible for someone to be screaming every time they open their mouth. Eventually she storms off. I don't know how long we stood there; because when you're staring at someone's forehead you lose track of time.

"No cases until twelve today," says Reto in the break room.

Today is Sunday and the doctors don't come in until twelve. They all go to church in the morning. Well, they all say they're going to church. Half go and the other half use it as an excuse to come in late.

It feels good to have a break from doing surgery. The last few days we've been loaded with them. We've been getting bombed at least twice a week, and that means we're overloaded.

Torres looks happy. This is his third day in a row on first shift so he's getting into a routine.

"Anthony, listen to what Reto was just telling me. You will never believe who got caught having sex."

I don't have to hear any more, I'm already laughing. Torres told me that in Guatemala everyone minds their own business and no one cares what anyone else is doing. But since he came to America, and specifically since he joined the Army, he loves to hear gossip; sex is usually the number one topic of discussion. It's probably because it seems to be the most taboo. People have sex, yet the military likes to pretend they don't. The Army does this to try and keep everyone under control. They want to run things like a well-oiled machine, and when sex is brought into the equation you bring in emotions; emotions have no place in a machine. I don't know whether it's because of the no-sex rule or in spite of the no-sex rule, but regardless, everyone still has sex and because of the rule they are forced to sneak around, which can often lead to hilarious circumstances. Like in Wisconsin when two soldiers got caught having sex in a Porta-Potty, and then two got caught having sex in a dumpster. I guess that's what happens when you try to control people—sex in a dumpster. Personally, I don't want to do that.

"Sergeant Cost got caught having sex yesterday in the TV room. And get this, it was in the afternoon, the door wasn't even locked, and it was First Sergeant Mardine who caught them."

Sergeant Cost is a short woman with thick glasses and a bowl hair cut. She is also mentally challenged. I'm not sure how she was even able to get in the Army. I think by some grace of God she did well on a test and the Army didn't even bother looking into what type of person she is, only her test score. She also has five children who are mentally challenged, some functionally, some not.

Here's a story about her: While we were at our pre-deployment training at Ft. McCoy, Cost called her kids back home—

"Listen honey, Daddy doesn't love you. That's why he broke up with mommy. Put your brother on the phone. Hey baby, listen, no, don't put your Daddy on the phone, he's a bad man. I don't know why your sister's crying. It's probably because she realized that your father doesn't love you guys. I love you, though. Okay, talk to you later."

First Sergeant Mardine overheard Cost on the phone and immediately ran over to her. "You can't talk to your kids like that! It could emotionally scar them for life!" Cost just looked at her as if she was crazy to tell her how to parent her children.

First Sergeant Mardine is just below the rank of command sergeant major—she's in charge of the enlisted soldiers for our unit.
Even though she's in her late sixties, she has more fire in her than
ninety percent of the people in the unit. She's tiny, 5'4", but she's
built like an ox, strong and thick. She has been in the Army for
over thirty years, and it's obvious that those years have toughened
her up. She has puffy white hair shaped into a male hair cut—high
and tight. I guess the hair cut fits, though, because she's a lesbian.

Torres is still talking: "First Sergeant Mardine really wants
Cost strung up. I heard she's going to give her extra duty and loss
of pay for a month."

I realize First Sergeant Mardine can be quite vindictive and
overly dramatic. Extra duty and loss of a month's pay, just for having sex?

"Do you think they're just trying to send a message, since she's
the first one to get caught having sex and the Army doesn't want
us having sex?" I say to no one in particular.

Torres starts laughing.

BAANNGGG!

The noise is loud but it's not a mortar. It's a gunshot. It's close,
maybe even in the hospital. We jump up and run toward the front
of the hospital where the noise came from.

A small group of people are gathered around the front door
looking out. Sergeant Elster walks through the door. He looks
confused. His head is hanging low and he's holding his weapon at
a weird angle, cocked to the left and down at the floor. He just had
an accidental discharge.

At the front of our hospital there are two armed guards and
two metal barrels filled with sand. Before going into the hospital, everyone must put the nozzle of their weapon into the barrel,
pull back the charging handle, and show that the inside chamber
of their weapon is empty of bullets. Then you pull the trigger to
prove that there are no bullets. Once the guards check to make

sure that the chamber is empty, the person is allowed to enter the hospital. Most of the time the guards are tired, bored, and don't pay close attention. I know what happened: Elster was coming off a guard duty shift, something that anyone below a sergeant rank has to go through.

(Every seven to ten days, everyone has to do a day of guard duty. It consists of six hours on duty, six hours off duty, six hours on duty, six hours off duty, and then back to the regular schedule of work in the hospital.)

Elster was tired from being on guard duty so he didn't pay attention when he locked his weapon to the rear. The guards were tired from being on duty and they didn't pay attention. Elster pulled the trigger and fired a round into the barrel. With the crazy hours we are working in the OR, it was only a matter of time until something like this happened. Luckily, though, it was only into a barrel of sand and not a fellow soldier.

Elster walks by us and toward the commander's office for disciplinary action.

WEEK 3, DAY 7, IRAQ

0700 HOURS, OR

We have three injuries on the way: two amputees and a GSW, all Iraqi civilians. When the patients arrive, I'm working in the one-bed OR to perform an amputation. We cut his arm off and on each leg give him an external fixator (ex-fix)—a type of instrument we use for broken bones. We put a drill on either side of the broken bone connected with a carbon pole; it's like a child's toy.

1520 HOURS, OR

When I get out of surgery I notice that Crade, Chandler, and Reto are all in the main OR talking to Torres. This is strange because we usually talk in the break room. I wonder why they're all out here in the main OR. I turn and see that the break room door is closed.

"What's everyone doing out here?" I ask as I sit down with the group.

Crade looks at me.

"Gagney had to come in to deal with Elster's accidental discharge of his weapon. When he did, Captain Tarr saw him and started yelling. She was shaking and her whole face was red. Then Hudge and I came in, and Gagney, Hudge, and Captain Tarr all went to the break room to talk."

"What's her problem this time?" I ask.

"She's yelling at him because of Torres." Crade points at Torres.

Torres laughs uncomfortably. "Well, Captain Tarr was our nurse in surgery today. I asked her for an instrument but she gave me the wrong one so the doctor yelled at her. She told him that I asked her for the wrong one."

The break room door bursts opens and Gagney walks out. His face is beet red and it looks like steam is rising from his bald spot. He storms out of the OR. Captain Tarr walks out and she's redder than Gagney. Tears are streaming down her cheeks and her hands are shaking.

Hudge walks out; her cheeks look pink. "You guys will not believe what just happened," she says, almost laughing.

"Tarr pulls Gagney and me into a meeting and I have no idea what's going on. Tarr is making no sense; she's yelling and her entire body turns red: face, neck, hands, and arms and her whole body starts shaking uncontrollably."

What none of us immediately knew was that Captain Tarr had been broken. Being in war is a true test of character. First I blow up at Waters and now Tarr is losing it. Everyone has their breaking point, the only question is who will reach theirs first. Only time will tell if Tarr's able to pick herself up and move on.

WEEK 4, DAY 1, IRAQ

1500 HOURS, OR

The next patients come in: One is an American soldier and one an Iraqi insurgent. The Iraqi is someone our guys have been trying to find for a long time. Only minutes earlier both had been trying to kill one another—now they're lying next to each other.

In my mind I can see the families and friends of both victims. They would begin to pray for them, praying for the death of the other, saying as long as their son "didn't die in vain" it would be okay.

Hudge is in the single OR, so Crade and I have to do surgery on the American and Iraqi in the double OR.

Crade is twenty-two—two years older than me—thirty pounds overweight, and has a baby face that makes him look about thirteen. Tattoos of satanic symbols cover both of his arms. A few months ago, I saw him reading the *Satanic Bible* by Anton Szandor

LaVey. He tried to convince me to read it with him, telling me that I'd get a lot out of it. But I turned him down because of something my eighth-grade health teacher said a long time ago. She told me that if someone ever asks me to worship Satan, politely say, "No thank you." So that's what I said to Crade. "No thank you." He told me he's dating a specialist from the mental health section, but he won't tell me her name. He also has an ex-girlfriend back home who is pregnant with his child, but that's all he says—he doesn't like to talk about it. Even though I think it's a little freaky that he worships Satan, he's my friend; I love him.

I'm working on the Iraqi. Both patients, sworn enemies, look so fragile and vulnerable next to each other.

"Scalpel!" Dr. Bill yells.

It takes me out of my daze. I shake my head and get back to work.

Two men walk into the room, joined by Captain Tarr. All are gowned up in the proper sterile medical gear: hat, scrubs, and mask. One of the men is carrying an expensive camera. He is young and has long black hair pulled back in a ponytail. The other man looks older and tall. He doesn't look happy as he writes on a note pad.

I look over at Dr. Bill.

"They're from the *Boston Globe*."

We finish our surgeries and both of the patients leave the OR—alive.

MONTH 2

"...I HATE
THE ARMY
AND WISH
I'D NEVER
JOINED."

WEEK 1, DAY 1, IRAQ

2230 HOURS, MY ROOM

Beep. Beep. Beep. Beep. Beep.

I'm tired. I don't want to get up. I want a day off. It's now the beginning of month two and I feel as though I can no longer hide the insanity. The constant change in sleeping patterns is really starting to take its toll. I can visibly see how the shift changes are affecting all of us in the unit. Denti chain-smokes and has heavy, dark bags under his eyes. Crade has gained weight and spends his day drinking coffee and snapping at everyone. I can't remember seeing Reto and Torres for days or weeks. During surgery I spend my time chewing gum to try and keep from falling asleep as my head bobs up and down. The doctors all think I'm a slacker because I keep dozing off. I see the first-shift doctors every third day. They all assume I only work every third day and have two days off. The doctors and nurses don't know we change shifts every day so they say nothing. This is the Army; we can't complain.

I have a different sleeping pattern every day. On the days that I do fall sleep, mortars constantly interrupt me. Yesterday or I think it was yesterday, I worked eleven hours and fifteen minutes. I know it was eleven hours and fifteen minutes because everyone else only worked eight hours and I keep track. I came home after work and fell asleep. Three hours later we were under a mortar attack. I grabbed my weapon and ran to a bunker. An hour later the base was all clear and we were told there was a mass casualty. After sitting around, we are told there really was no mass casualty and to go back to our rooms. Two and a half hours later I wake up and lie in bed thinking about everything that just happened. My sleep is no longer natural. When I lay my head down to sleep every night I am exhausted but I can't fall asleep. I can't get any sleep. My body isn't getting used to the changing shifts. It doesn't know when I'm supposed to be awake, so I take pills to make it sleep.

When I first started taking the pills I had to wait two days for the store to get more in—they're always sold out of sleeping pills. I'm not the only one with this problem. I only took half a pill the first time. Now I have to take two and a half. I know that I shouldn't be taking that much, but I can't sleep. The pills make my body sleep, but because of my constant fear of the mortar attacks and shift changes, my mind doesn't. My mind continues to race and I think about home. I think about why I'm fighting this war and my eyes tear up. I think of all the people we've killed. I think of all the people's families—mothers, fathers, siblings—and how they'll never see them again. I think of my parents, brothers, and sisters worrying about me. I think about my friends, all of them living their lives as if I've never existed—these are all the mediocre nights.

Sometimes I go into the hospital and have to do surgery just as the sleeping pills begin to kick in. I spend the rest of the night pinching myself and throwing cold water on my face. At night I tell myself it's not worth it. I tell myself I hate the Army and wish I'd never joined. I curse the war on both sides, American and Iraqi. I wish everyone would just . . . die . . . so that I could go home.

Other nights I lie in bed and think about everything and anything, and the only thing I can feel is nothing. I think about the war and I feel nothing. I think about life and death, mine and everyone else's, and I feel nothing. I think about myself and I don't care if I live or die. On these nights, mortars go off and I won't get out of bed. I'll lie in bed as the bombs go off. I tell myself it doesn't matter if I live or die, nothing matters—I like it when I feel nothing.

"Hey man, you just going to lie in bed, or you going to get up for work?" my roommate Markham asks. "Are you all right, man? I mean, seriously, you've been looking pretty bad lately." Markham sits up in bed as he looks at me. I can tell he cares, but today I feel nothing. I stare at him and keep silent. Then I sit up and put my socks on.

"I don't know if you know it or not, but you were talking in your sleep last night. You started yelling at me. You didn't know what time of the day it was, what day, or when you were supposed to be working."

I look at Markham and wish that today wasn't a day where I felt nothing but apathy. I wish it was a nice, caring day; one where I could sit down and talk with him about all my fears and concerns about fighting this war and missing everyone back home. I don't have the heart to tell him that I wasn't just talking in my sleep. I was wide awake and I really didn't know what day it was or if I had to be at work. That's how it's been for the last few days. During the surgeries, I can't remember if the surgery I just did happened the day before or only a few hours ago. The surgeries are routine and all blend into one another—pass this, pass that, cut here, cauterize there. The doctors and nurses don't care. As long as I pass the right instrument, what's it to them? They don't complain. I feel that being too good at my job is hurting me. I know that if I messed up a surgery just once I could blame it on the lack of sleep and Gagney would be in trouble. I know all I need is for one patient to die because an OR medic messed up due to lack of sleep. I know that one patient's death could force Gagney to have to make a new schedule.

Markham is staring at me. I don't know how long ago he stopped talking, but his face looks concerned. I've seen the look on his face before. I've seen it on the face of my older brothers every time I've gotten myself into trouble or a situation that was over my head. Markham wants to help me out. Why couldn't he have chosen a day to talk to me when I feel something? Why did he have to choose today when I feel nothing?

"All right, quit staring at me," I finally say. "Everything's fine." Markham continues staring at me as I get dressed for work. It makes me uncomfortable. I don't understand how he could care about me more than he cares about himself.

2300 HOURS, OR

I walk into the OR and Sergeants Waters and Sellers are standing there. There are only supposed to be two people on shift, but three of us are standing here. I don't know what's going on. I know that I'm on third shift today. I look back at Sellers and Waters; I know that Waters is on shift, so Sellers must be wrong or just here to hang out.

"Ummmm," Sellers says as she turns around and heads toward the break room and takes the schedule off of the door.

I grab the schedule from Sellers's hands as she begins reading it.

"FUCK!" I scream.

Sellers has the schedule flipped to a page showing three days. On one day I am working first shift, on another second, and the other third. I don't know what day today is.

"FUCK!" I scream again.

Waters, who has been a lot nicer to me since I yelled at her, leans over my shoulder and points at the right day.

I let the schedule drop out of my hands and I turn around to head back to my room. The sleeping pills have worn off and my screaming woke me up. It's 2300 hours. I need to be at work in eight hours and I am wide awake.

2315 HOURS, MY ROOM

Markham is already asleep and snoring when I get back to my room. Opening the door, I slam it closed and turn the light on. I am angry, but I don't know what to do with the anger. I don't know what day of the week it is. I'm angry at Gagney and his schedules and most of all angry at myself for not being able to do anything. I'm powerless—I'm weak—I'm not a man—I only do whatever I am told—I'm a sprocket in the machine of the Army, an easily replaceable sprocket. I wish I could go back to feeling nothing. I know what to do with nothing—nothing. I know what to do with nothing—nothing. I know what to do with nothing—nothing. . . .

I glance over at the bottle of pills on my nightstand. It's the middle of the night. I'm nowhere near sleep and I have eight hours to kill. I really have no choice but to take more. . . .

WEEK 1, DAY 2, IRAQ

0730 HOURS, OR

Gagney is at the door waiting for me as I head into the OR half an hour late:

"Hey Anthony, I heard you came in last night by accident. I hope I'm not working you too hard, am I? How you feeling buddy?" He smiles, but it looks awkward and forced. I think the only thing scarier than seeing your executioner would be seeing your executioner smile as he kills you. Gagney talks to me through his smile.

"I went to the Post Exchange and got everyone bagels. Go ahead and grab one."

Elster and Reto are in the break room eating.

"So, I'm in Iraq and I no longer dream of being home with family or friends. Now I only dream of Gagney being nice to me," I say in an attempt at humor.

"You ain't dreaming," Elster tells me. "Gagney *is* being nice to you."

The chief ward masters are having a meeting with us today. Chief ward masters are the ones that are in charge of the hospital. If there are any problems, they're the final word. Early this morning someone went and complained about Gagney and the way he's been running things. Apparently, our section looks like crap. All the other sections are on set schedules and ours is the only one that changes every day.

The day goes by slow. We have no cases so Gagney has us clean the entire OR. He sends Reto to tell everyone on all the other shifts about the meeting. It's going to be between first and second shift, but everyone from third shift has to be there as well.

1505 HOURS, OR

The chief ward masters ask us to tell them what's bothering us.

Torres is the first to start talking. "I'm not one to complain, but the way this man is treating us is disrespectful—"

"Idiots, he treats us like we're idiots," Hudge interrupts.

"We switch shifts every day. I am on second shift today. Yesterday I was on first, the day before that second, the day before that third. Tomorrow I'm back on third shift. How does any of that make sense?" says Crade.

"He doesn't do any work. All he does is sit around and play computer games and watch anime. He was sent here as an operating room technician, but why has he only done a handful of cases since he's been here? I do as many in one day as he does in a month," says Sellers, who has obviously come to see the light.

Waters jumps in. "We need better leadership, someone who will stay on top of things. He yelled at me twice last week over nothing. There is no need for him to raise his voice to us."

An hour goes by and everyone has something negative to say about Gagney. Hudge, Sellers, and Waters all have tears in their eyes. The chief ward masters look at Reto and me and ask if we have anything to add since we haven't spoken yet. Everyone in the OR is looking at us. I look at Reto. His eyes are red, not from the lack of sleep, but because he's going to cry. He can't control himself any longer.

"This is bullshit. I joined the Army to help people, not to be treated like shit. I understand that we're at war and that times are tough. But look at every other section. . . ." Reto has to stop to compose himself. "Every other section in this hospital is running fine. Gagney won't even let us try and change the schedule to get a better one. We mentioned it and he told us just to deal with it. He's a fucking. . . ." Reto stops talking. He knows he can't talk without crying. Everyone turns and looks at me.

I look back at them.

"I agree with Reto," I say.

Everyone continues to look at me and I look back. Waters, Sellers, and Hudge look angrily at me, but I look back at them and with my eyes I try to explain that my body won't let me feel. I have nothing to say because I can't speak with the passion that they all just spoke with. I wish I could stand up and give a moving speech that would change our entire section and make us all friends and love each other, but I know I can't do this and if I could it would be all lies. I really can't stand up for myself. I know it's best for me to just sit here in silence.

The chief ward masters look at me as if I'm slow. I stare at their foreheads and they get up and say that they'll deal with the problem. When I get up, Waters seems especially disappointed that I haven't said anything. As I leave to go back toward my room, I overhear everyone trying to figure out who it was that complained to the chief ward masters. When I get back to my room I leave a note on Markham's pillow: "Thank You."

WEEK 1, DAY 3, IRAQ

0640 HOURS, OR

I walk in early; I know I can't be late two days in a row. Gagney is already in. He's sitting at a desk and all around him are crumpled up pieces of yellow paper.

I get my room ready for surgery. There are four scheduled.

1500 HOURS, OR

When I get out of surgery the second shift comes in. Gagney is still sitting at the desk surrounded by even more pieces of crumpled yellow paper. He smiles when he sees Hudge:

"Sergeant Hudge, would you please come to the break room with me for a second?"

Two minutes later Gagney comes out lookin' free as a bird, grabs his coat and weapon, and leaves. Hudge walks over to me with a smile from ear to ear.

"Gagney wants me to rewrite the schedule."

1700 HOURS, OR

Crade has a copy of Hudge's finished schedule.

First Shift: Gagney—Shift leader; Elster—In charge of supply; Crade—In charge of CMS (central material services, the place where we sterilize instruments.); Anthony, Chandler, Torres—Main OR technicians.

Second Shift: Hudge—Shift leader; Reto, Denti—Main OR technicians.

Third Shift: Waters—Shift leader; Sellers—Main OR technician.

It's mapped out for the next month. Hudge has our official days off scheduled, taking into consideration guard duty, so that when it's complete, we'll get the next day off. Bottom line: Every eleven days we'll have a day off.

Everyone is ecstatic, even the ones that weren't changing shifts in the first place—Waters, Elster, Hudge. Gagney walks in and notices the commotion. He studies the schedule and quickly throws it on the table. When he storms off, Hudge laughs.

"He asks me to make the schedule because he said that everyone can't be happy. He figured everyone would be mad at me instead of him. . . . It only took me half an hour."

All we needed was a half-hour to make all the pains of the last month go away.

WEEK 1, DAY 4, IRAQ

0600 HOURS, MY ROOM

The new shift: Everyone is in a great mood when I arrive at work.

"Hey Anthony," Gagney says enthusiastically as I enter the OR. His overly friendly, almost gay voice kind of freaks me out, but I brush it off. Today is a good day and I don't feel like thinking about the inner thoughts behind everyone's actions.

"Can you do me a favor?" Gagney asks, which is the first time I have ever heard him ask for something and not demand it. My ears perk up and I know that I am now obligated to do it no matter what, simply for the reason because he is asking and not ordering.

"Can you go tell everyone from all shifts to come in at fifteen hundred hours? And after you tell everyone you can go back to your room and have the rest of the day off. Take a break, here's my pager. If there's an emergency I'll get in touch with you."

I know I am not dreaming. I tell everyone to be in at 1500 hours.

1505 HOURS, OR

Gagney is talking to us:

"I know that things haven't been easy this past month. I know that I may have been hard on a few of you, but after talking to the chief ward masters and seeing how easily Hudge was able to make that schedule, I realize that I may need to back off a little bit and become more of a reasonable and approachable leader. So if you guys have any further complaints, bring them up to me first. There's no need to go over my head to the chief ward masters. In fact, and I shouldn't even have to order this, but you are not allowed to go directly to the chief ward masters. You can talk to them and complain about me to them, but you are ordered to come to me first," says Gagney.

Gagney finishes and leaves. We all know that he can't stop us from contacting the chief ward masters and that we don't have to tell him, but it's not worth getting into.

WEEK 2, DAY 1, IRAQ

1600 HOURS, MY ROOM

"You're not going to believe this!" Denti yells as he barges into my room. We're supposed to go to the gym but not for another ten minutes.

"Ah, what the hell, man. Knock next time." I'm naked and changing into my clothes.

"It happened in the southern hospital."

I put my underwear on as quickly as possible.

"This thing is huge."

I'm looking around the room for clean socks.

Here's what he was telling me:

"When our unit went to Iraq, we split up. Half of the people went to run our hospital and half of our people went to run another hospital in the southern part of Iraq.

"Staff Sergeant North was on mailroom duty and it was slow, so he decides for fun to open up someone's mail and start reading it. He's just sitting there reading somebody else's mail, and the next thing you know the guy whose mail he's reading actually walks in and catches him.

"The guy starts yelling at North for reading *his* mail, and North just turns white as a ghost. He realizes that this guy is only a specialist, though, so North says that he shouldn't be talking to a superior officer that way.

"The guy then goes to his chain of command and tries to file a complaint against our unit and North. His commanders are outraged. But since the soldier and the rest of his unit are all leaving in two weeks, the commanders don't want to waste their time with complaints. They just want to go home. The soldier then talks to the unit that's replacing his, and they don't want to file a complaint against a unit either, bad politics and all.

"So this guy wants to file a complaint but no one will do it for him. No one wants to cause trouble. Eventually the guy decides to go to the IG (inspector general) himself.

"It then comes out that we have more complaints against us than any other unit in Iraq. I guess a bunch of people from our unit and other units complained about us when we were in Wisconsin and since we've been in Iraq.

"So the Good Ol' Boys hear about the complaint and they're livid."

Okay, the Good Ol' Boys (GOBs for short):

They're a degenerate group of colonels and generals who, while in Wisconsin we ate rotten food, they ate at fancy restaurants and joked with each other, saying, "Let them eat cake." These are the men who slept in two-man rooms while we slept in thirty-man bays. They get chauffeured around base while we walk everywhere. They also allow people in our unit to do whatever they want as long as they don't get caught. They're going to lead us into battle.

Colonel Tucker is the leader of the gang. The only way to describe him would be: a mad Russian scientist, without the charisma. Tucker's main lackey is our unit command sergeant major, Command Sergeant Major (CSM) Ridge. Ridge is the man in charge of the enlisted section of our unit. He's in his sixties, well over six feet tall, and has white cropped hair with the standard high-and-tight military haircut. Ridge is also an alcoholic. Even though we were not permitted to drink alcohol while on base in Wisconsin (or once we get to Iraq for that matter), Ridge has already been caught illegally drinking several times. He'll most likely never get in trouble, though, because of his connections and rank.

"Anyway, I guess this kid's complaint was the one that broke the camel's back. The Good Ol' Boys have a meeting down south and order all sergeants and above to attend. They tell CSM Ridge to have the meeting and tell everyone that they don't want any more complaints being filed against our unit from within our unit. If they do, they'll be reprimanded. CSM Ridge calls the meeting . . . but get this. He's drunk at the meeting. No one is allowed to drink in this entire goddamned country and this guy is totaled. He says that if anyone files a complaint against the unit or specifically him, he'll get them shipped to a frontline unit where they might not make it back."

It also turns out that the meeting wasn't just about us having the most complaints. In Wisconsin, after our initial climate control meeting, which gauged how well our commanders were doing as leaders, a few people contacted the inspector general. We had some problems with morale, conduct, control, and chain of command. Other than that we were fine. It actually started when two of the highest-ranking people in our unit said that if this were Vietnam, someone would commit fratricide the moment we stepped in Iraq. Fratricide means to deliberately shoot at someone who's on the same team as you. So this one colonel, who looks like Geraldo Rivera, is actually suggesting we shoot our commanders (the GOBs). The other colonel, a frail old woman in her seventies, stands up and says mutiny would be a good idea as well. She implied that she might take control of the unit. Almost everyone at the meeting stands up and gives the two colonels a standing ovation and a round of applause.

The major who was conducting the meeting then went ballistic: "You people cannot be serious! You are going to war in two weeks, and you're applauding the idea of mutiny and fratricide?"

Since then there have been even more complaints. We are actually under an official investigation by the inspector general.

WEEK 3, DAY 1, IRAQ

2200 HOURS, MY ROOM

I'm beginning to like Markham more and more. We've been roommates for two months, and we're finally starting to hit it off. He's a skilled guitar player, and even though he's twelve years older than me, I feel as though we connect.

"Hey, you heard about the mail fraud and how our unit's under investigation?"

Maybe it has to do with my family, maybe I feel more comfortable around older people than those my own age: I grew up with four older brothers and two older sisters. All my brothers and one sister ended up joining the military, but in different branches. As a child, I heard stories of intense military training during the day and parties that lasted all night. I grew up watching military movies and playing GI Joe in my backyard. So when I turned seventeen the question never seemed to be if I would join the military or go to college. It was only which branch of the military will it be. Markham is the opposite of me; he has younger brothers. When I thanked him about the schedule issues with Gagney, he told me it's what he would have done for someone in his family.

"The rest of the story involves that new girl that you said was cute, Sergeant Thurbid, and that guy in charge of the OR down south, Sergeant Plown."

My curiosity is piqued as Markham continues to divulge the news of the day. Thurbid is a soldier who recently got sent up to us from our southern hospital, and I briefly mentioned to Markham that I thought she was cute. I may never hear the end of it, but I'm tired and could use a good bedtime story.

"First off, I will say this. I am not from this damn unit. I was cross-leveled into it. I'm from Washington State. All this drama that goes on is always because of you damn New Englanders," Markham says.

I laugh knowing he's wrong because Captain Tarr is from his home state and she's got her own bag of drama, but I don't say this and instead I tell him to go on.

"So a few weeks ago that meeting went down with CSM Ridge. Well, when the speech was going on Sergeant Plown was taking notes. He wrote down everything that CSM Ridge said. He then typed up an anonymous letter and mailed it to every congressman in the U.S. The IG heard about the letter and started a new investigation into our unit. A general even went down south to personally check up on our unit, and he brought with him a few CID soldiers to conduct the investigation."

The CID is the Criminal Investigation Division, kind of like a military FBI.

Markham picks up his guitar and starts strumming as he tells the story. I enjoy it. Even though what he's telling me isn't the most pleasant, the sound of the guitar in the background can make even the worst story sound relaxing.

"The GOBs are not pleased about the IG investigating them again. The next day, they're in the dining facility with Ridge having dinner and discussing how to get everyone in our unit to stop contacting the IG. They want to find a way to order us to do it without actually ordering—which is illegal. And here's the part you're not going to believe."

"While the GOBs and CSM Ridge are having this discussion at the dining facility, they don't realize it but sitting behind them are three members of the CID who are part of the investigation against us. They hear their whole conversation."

Markham stops playing guitar and begins tapping his cigarette pack against his palm. He's craving a cigarette, I can tell. So I get out of bed and we head outside.

He hands me a cigarette. I pause. I know I shouldn't—I've already had ten this week—but I light one up with Markham anyway, and he continues talking and playing his guitar.

2230 HOURS, OUTSIDE

All right, I'm listening to Markham:

"The IG does their investigation for a few days, gathers all the information they need, and then heads back to their headquarters to make a decision on what to do—if anything. So everyone leaves, except for one CID guy who is tasked to stay behind and investigate the charges of North reading someone's mail. Oh yeah, I forgot to tell you. The GOBs found out that Plown was the one who wrote the letter to the senators. They fired him from his position as head of the OR and now he's working in the administrative section of the unit down south. This way they can keep an eye on him. But anyways, back to the mail fraud story. . . . So here's really why your cutie Sergeant Thurbid got sent up here: Staff Sergeant North approached her:

'Thurbid, listen, I need you to do me a favor. I've been having some trouble with this guy. He's trying to get me in big trouble for reading his mail. My whole career could be ruined because of this guy.'

"Thurbid looks at North. They've been friends for years. She has three kids and Staff Sergeant North and his wife, Captain Dillon, even babysat for them a few times."

'I know; that's awful.'

'This is a big favor and I understand if you'll say no, but this scandal could ruin both me and my wife's career. I could even go to jail. The specialist who filed the complaint is kind of a dork, but he's been here a long time. I was thinking that if you slept with him you could then convince him to drop the charges.'

"So Thurbid thought it over. 'Okay, but you owe me . . . ,' she says."

Markham stops telling the story and puts his guitar down. He looks me in the eye.

"Now here's the best part of the story. . . . Thurbid has sex with the guy, and while they're having sex they decide to get a little freaky. Thurbid lets the guy give it to her in the ass with no condom. Then after the guy is done she sucks his dick. The next day she has an infection in and around her mouth. She goes to the hospital assuming it's some type of STD but is relieved when the doctor tells her it's only an E. coli infection. When Staff Sergeant North comes to visit her, he has no idea what to say at first, but then he gets a plan. Later that day she goes to the guy and says that he gave her an STD and that if he doesn't drop the claim against Staff Sergeant North that she'll file a complaint against him. The guy says he doesn't have an STD and tells her to go ahead. The guy then says that he knows that she and North are friends and it's obvious what they were trying to do, and that if she does tell, he'll get them both in trouble for blackmail."

I stare at Markham with my mouth wide open. This kind of stuff just doesn't happen back home. We finish up our cigarettes and head back into our room.

2300 HOURS, MY ROOM

"Staff Sergeant North and Thurbid were pissed. Their plan didn't work and she ended up having diarrhea and vomiting for a few days. Meanwhile the CID guy is still doing the investigation and is digging up more dirt on Staff Sergeant North. However, North and Thurbid concoct another brilliant plan. A few days later she's better and the infection is gone, and she seduces the CID guy, too. I kid you not. She starts sleeping with him.

"Oh, I almost forgot; as this is going on there's another scandal happening. First Sergeant Powell, from down south, is sleeping with a female soldier, but she's also sleeping with another soldier named Specialist Rubino. A week later Rubino finds out and starts a fight with Powell. Rubino is drunk and pushes Powell. They both start yelling at each other, and Rubino grabs Powell by the collar and pulls him to the ground. Staff Sergeant North hears the commotion and so does the CID guy—who comes running out of Thurbid's room—and they come running and break up the fight. Rubino gets arrested and Powell walks away scot-free, even though he shouldn't have been sleeping with someone in his chain of command. And speaking of scot-free, the IG does its investigation and says the way our unit is being run is appalling at best and illegal at worst. But—and this is the Army for you—they also say that although they know illegal things are going on, they can't actually prove any of it. Still, the GOBs decide they need fall guys, just as a sign of good faith that they're changing things. So Rubino was demoted to private and that's when they sent Thurbid up here."

"The GOBs also needed someone to blame for the conversation that was heard in the dining facility and where Ridge threatened to send people to a frontline unit if they complained."

I look at Markham. I nod yes.

"Well, CSM Fellows, from down south, objected to having the meeting in the first place. He knew it was illegal to order us not to report complaints and he told that to the GOBs. They ignored him then, but now they're blaming everything on him and they also sent him to us."

Markham picks up his guitar and starts talking about something else. I actually feel bad for Command Sergeant Major Fellows. I liked him. He's short, stocky, and smokes such big cigars that he'd give Freud a phallic complex. He always seemed to be trying to sell you something and to make a quick buck. Now he's working in the OR as an anesthesiologist technician, a job usually done by some twenty-year-old specialist. All because he stood up and said that we should have the right to voice our opinions about our leadership.

I take two melatonin sleeping pills. Nothing happens and after a while I take two more. Slowly I drift off.

What an outfit: people in their thirties, married with children, all of them having affairs. One was a heroin addict; the other has slept with eleven men in the past three months. One guy tried to kill himself and another kidnapped a drug dealer. Alcoholics, chain smokers, compulsive gamblers—who am I to judge?

Maybe it wasn't such a good bedtime story after all. I don't want to imagine what types of dreams I'm going to have tonight. They'll probably involve some big, sweaty man with an E. coli infection. . . .

WEEK 3, THANKSGIVING DAY, IRAQ

1130 HOURS, DINING FACILITY

I'll give the Army credit for one thing: they know how to do Thanksgiving. Turkey, ham, fish, mashed potatoes, corn, peas, carrots, squash, corn bread, apple pie, and blueberry pie. Torres even found a flier about the Dallas Cowboy cheerleaders, who are on base signing autographs. "I was actually in one of these programs down in Texas called Adopt-a-Soldier," I'm telling Torres as we go through the food line. "I was doing my operating room training. It was Thanksgiving and we weren't allowed to go home, so the Army started this program where families could take two soldiers home with them for Thanksgiving and have them eat dinner with their families."

Torres and I make our way to an empty table. He's trying to balance all of the food on his tray and he's not listening. I just keep on talking, though.

"There were thousands of us down there for training and we were certain that there was no way we'd all get families to go home with. We knew somebody would get stuck, and we'd have to eat at the D-fac. It was like freshman gym class all over again, some will get picked and some won't. But there ended up being too many families; the Army had to turn away hundreds saying they didn't have enough soldiers to go around. Thousands of families were waiting to pick us up and take us to their house for a home-cooked meal. Absolutely, it was one of the best Thanksgivings I ever had."

Torres stops eating for a second and laughs.

"What are you trying to say Anthony, that you want an Iraqi family to take you home today?"

WEEK 4, DAY 1, IRAQ

0700 HOURS, OR

Denti and I are in the break room having lunch when Gagney kicks open the door.

"WHO THE FUCK DID IT! WHEN I FIND OUT—YOU HAVE GOT TO BE FUCKING KIDDING ME. . . ."

Denti and I sit there staring at each other, bracing ourselves.

"WHO WENT TO THE CHIEF WARD MASTERS—YOU TELL ME, ANTHONY!"

"I don't—"

"DON'T FUCKING PLAY DUMB WITH ME—"

He starts pacing back and forth, mumbling under his breath.

"IT'S A MILITARY CRIME TO GO OVER YOUR CHAIN OF COMMAND'S HEAD! YOU NEVER SAW ME TREAT A SOLDIER THAT WAY."

Denti and I are staring at the ground.

"TELL THAT TO HUDGE."

Reto comes around the corner, after Gagney leaves. We explain the shit storm that just happened.

0720 HOURS, OR

"I'm the one that went to the chief ward masters," Reto says. "Hudge and I were on second shift and Gagney stops by last night. He forgot his computer game. Hudge decides it was a good time to talk about some of our complaints—the ones we talked about at the meeting. He starts screaming at her in the break room—I can hear it. He doesn't think we've got any problems; he thinks she's making it up. He tells her that people make fun of her behind her back. He tells her she's stupid and she's a liar and she has no idea what she's doing.

"I got her husband from the ER, she was crying. I went to the chief ward masters' office and told them. Hudge doesn't know any of it."

I look at Reto and for the first time I feel respect for one of my fellow soldiers.

0730 HOURS, OR

I chuckle to myself. All it took for me to respect someone in the military was for that person to refuse a direct order. Reto was ordered—we were all ordered—by Gagney not to complain about him, but here Reto has refused to play the game and went ahead with what he thinks is right. Refusing an order takes a lot more courage than following one—I know that. I'm a little scared for him because I realize that if Gagney finds out it's Reto, he'll crucify him.

"Last night I went to the chief ward masters' office and told them everything about what happened between you and Gagney."

Hudge looks at Reto and me. She thinks he's kidding.

Reto nods his head.

"Oh, my God."

"Yeah, well. . . . "

"That was really nice of you. . . ."

Hudge smiles and hugs Reto.

"That's not the whole story," I say, bringing the room down. "Basically, Gagney's not going to take it lying down."

The smile leaves Hudge's face.

Reto starts talking.

"Don't worry; we've got your back. Everything will be fine, and if anyone's going to get in trouble it won't be you. But you should probably see the chaplain or mental health officer. Just let them know what's going on, because they're the ones who usually intervene in these types of situations, that's really the best thing to do."

If you could have only seen Reto talking to Hudge like that. She tells him she just wishes that everyone could forget the whole thing.

WEEK 4, DAY 2, IRAQ

0700 HOURS, HOSPITAL

The chief ward masters can't believe what they hear. Until Reto talked to them, they'd thought for sure their little meeting solved all of our problems. Gagney gets called into their office—and he gets reprimanded for being cruel to Hudge. For three days, he's felt great bringing her down. Now he doesn't know what hit him, and he's the one getting yelled at. It's just like Gagney, though: He loves to make people feel bad, but every single time he does it, he can't even help it, he gets in trouble. It's like a dog that loves jumping on the couch but is slapped every time he tries to do it. What happens with the dog, though, is eventually the dog's owners get tired of telling it no and just say "screw it" and let the dog jump on the couch.

0800 HOURS, HOSPITAL

Gagney gets out of the meeting with the chief ward masters and walks in the opposite direction of the OR.

1400 HOURS, HOSPITAL

Gagney has another meeting with the chief ward masters.

1500 HOURS, OR

Hudge enters the break room as Reto and I are playing our first game of Rummy 500. She doesn't realize it, but Gagney is right behind her. He leans down, whispers something in her ear, and walks out of the room. She gives us a quick glance and follows him.

1630 HOURS, OR

Reto and I are finishing up our second game. I'm about to lay down my final cards when Hudge walks in the room.

"Well . . . the chief ward masters had three meetings with Gagney in the past two days. One yesterday, one this morning, then another one this afternoon. After the morning meeting he went and talked to the chaplain and the mental health officer."

Hudge stops and looks at Reto. She's looking to see if he had anything to do with it, since he mentioned the chaplain and mental health officer the day before. (The chaplain is an all-encompassing pastor for soldiers of every religion. A mental health officer is the Army's version of a psychiatrist.)

Reto shakes his head and puts his hands in the air to say that he didn't have anything to do with it. Hudge sounds frantic because she's speaking so fast, but she still has a slight smile on her face.

"Gagney orders me to go see them, so I head over to the chaplain's office." The smile leaves Hudge's face as she begins describing what happened:

"Come in, come in, I've been expecting you," the chaplain says eagerly.

"Sergeant Gagney told me to come speak to you. I'm not sure what this is about. . . ."

"Yes, yes, I spoke to Sergeant Gagney earlier this morning. Good man. We had a long talk, and I must admit a lot of it was about you."

"Um, okay, what do you mean you had a long talk about me?"

"Well, I can't get into the whole conversation because I keep my confidences, but Sergeant Gagney told me you've been having some problems with anger and that he's afraid you may be depressed."

Hudge pauses at this part of the story. Reto and I are laughing. We can't believe what we're hearing. It has to be a joke.

Hudge says she doesn't even believe what she's saying took place.

"I just stared at the chaplain. I didn't know what to say. I couldn't believe it; the angriest man in our unit tells the chaplain that *I've* got an anger problem.

"He says that Gagney told him that I've been acting up, yelling at people, and that a lot of people have problems with me. I'm just staring at him in shock. I'm speechless. Then, all of a sudden, I started to feel this thing come over me. My body is heating up. I could hear my heart pounding in my chest. 'I've got the anger problem? *I've* got the anger problem? He told you that I have the anger problem? That is insane!' I'm yelling."

"No need to raise your voice, Sergeant Hudge. Sergeant Gagney is just concerned about you and I think he might be right," replied the chaplain.

"He only came in here so *I* couldn't come to you first. He blew up at *me* the other day. If I complain about him, it will only look like revenge."

"Sergeant Hudge, you need to stop raising your voice."

Hudge stops the story and lowers her head.

"He was talking to me like I was a lunatic and Gagney was a saint. My voice wasn't raised at all.

"I storm out of the chaplain's office after about twenty minutes of listening to this bullshit. Of course, not before he had a chance to give me pamphlets on suicide and depression." Hudge throws the pamphlets down on the table.

"So I went to the mental health office. I figured there I'd at least be able to tell my side of the story, but once I got there . . . they're doing the same thing."

"Sergeant Hudge, glad to see you. You look good. Can I get you a drink? How are you feeling? Are you all right? You look good."

"I'm all right. . . ."

"Good, good. I was expecting you. I'm not sure if you are aware of this, but Sergeant Gagney stopped by earlier to see me and I. . . ."

"Are you kidding me? This is harassment, this is bullsh. . . ."

"Sergeant Hudge, no need for any language. I know you've been having some problems and Sergeant Gagney is only trying to help. Maybe if we can just talk for a little while we can get to the bottom of what's bothering you and causing you to lash out at everyone. Sergeant Gagney and I just want to help."

"*He's* the one who's been going around to everyone and telling them I have an anger problem—"

"Sergeant Hudge, no need to yell. We're in the same room. Why do you think that you have a problem with anger?"

"I. Don't. Have. A. Problem. With. Anger. Gagney does! He's the one who has the problem. . . ."

"Let's not point fingers or call anyone names. I'm right here."

"This is a riot. We don't give Gagney enough credit. He's a genius. He's a fucking diabolical genius!" Reto is laughing uncontrollably.

"And here's the best part." Hudge goes on, the smile back on her face. "After I see mental health, now I'm really steaming, but I've still got to go see the chief ward masters. I go there and try to tell them about what happened and how Gagney tried to set me up.

"He went to the chaplain and mental health and told them that I have anger problems and that I'm depressed. . . ."

"Yes, we are aware that Sergeant Gagney talked to them. We suggested that he talk to them and that it might help. We're glad you both were able to work things out," the chief ward masters reply calmly.

"Work things out?! Work things out?! He lied to everyone, he lied to us all. He made me cry. . . . I'm the one who has to go see the chaplain. . . . THIS IS INSANE!"

"Sergeant Hudge, just before you came in here, the chaplain stopped by. He said he was concerned about you and thinks Sergeant Gagney might be right."

Hudge stops talking. Her cheeks are flushed.

"I have to go to the bathroom."

WEEK 4, DAY 3, IRAQ

0545 HOURS, GUARD DUTY, EAST GATE

"And you, soldier, you will be guarding the East Side Gate," Staff Sergeant Elwood says to me. He's the sergeant in charge of guard duty, and he always seems to be smiling, even at 0545 in the morning. We're way in the middle of nowhere at the far end of the airport. The gate is seldom used; it's only for incoming Iraqis who work on the base. The station is a tiny wooden box that has two doors and one window. Inside there's a desk but no chairs. The job is deceptively simple:

All we—I'm assigned with another specialist by the name of Boredo—have to do is check people's IDs.

Formerly active duty infantry, Boredo loves to tell stories of his unit fighting battles. He then joined the reserves to become a medic. Denti and Boredo are a little alike, although Boredo seems like a child who wants to look up to an adult for help.

0700 HOURS, GUARD DUTY, EAST GATE

It's only one hour into guard duty and I feel like shooting myself. Better yet, I feel like shooting Boredo. I have already seriously considered punching him in the face twice, but every time I look at him—and I see those deer-caught-in-the-headlights eyes—I feel bad. I just can't do it.

"So then my unit ended up killing like twenty terrorists. Honestly, there's no feeling like the feeling of taking a man's life. It makes you feel alive. If you ever get a chance you should go outside the gate and see what it's really like, when you're not in the safety of your little hospital," Boredo says. I try to be friendly and act like I'm interested, resisting the urge to slap him. I know all I've got to do is hit him once and he'll shut up.

"Really? So how many did you kill?" I say instead of punching him. This is like the tiniest room I've ever been in.

"Well . . . I wasn't really there—"

"You weren't there when you killed them?" They really should give us a bench or something.

"—with them."

"I'm sorry. With who?"

"Okay, this happened when I wasn't there; it was after I left my infantry unit and joined this one—"

"Oh."

"But I heard all the stories, it was intense. One time my unit was held up in this alley—"

"Ah, okay," I reply.

"Well anyways, man, one time my unit was held up in this alley as they're getting ambushed. . . . "

Punch him. . . . Do it now. . . .

2000 HOURS, GUARD DUTY, EAST GATE

It's 8 P.M. and Boredo and I are back on shift. We have been back on since 6 P.M.

". . . Then I ran into this burning building and pulled out five guys that were about to be executed. Well, I didn't so much as do it as one of the guys in my old unit did, but man, you've got to get out of the wire so you can experience that stuff."

"Have you ever actually been outside the gate yourself?"

"Well, no, but. . . ."

Hit him. . . .

✚

BAAAMMM. BAAAAMMMM. BAAAAMMMM. BOOOMMMM.

BUNKERS! BUNKERS! BUNKERS! is shouted over the loudspeaker. This is really happening. Boredo and I lock the doors of the gate and grab our gear: a bulletproof flak vest, Kevlar, weapon, gas mask, and radio.

We're under attack again. It's been happening so often that it now feels like part of our daily routine. Wake up, eat breakfast, go to work, eat lunch, have a mortar attack, mortar attack ends, eat dinner, go to sleep, then repeat. Lately all the mortar rounds have been hitting the edges of our base and not making it on base, but these rounds sound close. They're loud. I have never been on guard duty during a mortar attack before. We lock the door behind us and start running for bunkers. The closest ones are fifty yards away. All of our gear is cumbersome and hanging loose. It slows us down as we run. I accidentally drop my Kevlar. I stop but Boredo keeps running. I see another soldier running for the bunker. I quickly pick up my Kevlar and start running.

BAAAAAAMMMMMMM!!!!!!!

I see a flash of blue. The noise is so loud that my ears are ringing.

BAAAAAAMMMMMMM!!!!!!!

I see another flash of blue. The mortars are hitting close. I've never seen the light of one before. I run for my life because the mortars are only twenty yards away.

Bang. Bang. Bang. Bang.

I hear gunfire; it's just above my head. It's coming from an Albanian guard post that's twenty feet in the air. They're part of the multinational forces that are on our base. The Albanians are in charge of base defense, and their tower is just above my head. They're firing at something, but I can't see what.

I run faster. My heart is beating; I feel alive. I feel like this is what life is meant to feel like. I have a goal of getting to the bunker, and I am using all my might and force to get there. I run and use every bit of energy my body has and it feels . . . great.

When I get to the bunker, Boredo and Staff Sergeant Elwood—the one who always smiles—are already there.

"I think that was the closest I've ever been to a mortar going off. I mean the closest without being in a bunker. We better get a CAB badge for this," says Elwood.

Boredo lights up at the mention of this.

A CAB badge is a Combat Action Badge—they're awarded to medical personnel for being in a combat situation. Elwood and Boredo are getting as excited as kids on Christmas morning because they think they'll qualify. The award isn't given for being in a bunker when mortars are hitting around you. You need to be within twenty-five yards of an unprotected area. Since we weren't in the bunkers when they started to hit, we qualify.

I'm trying to catch my breath as they yammer on, anxiously awaiting the ALL CLEAR from the loudspeaker.

Boredo is getting out of control. He now can tell a war story that he's actually in. "That was sooo intense. I can't wait to tell the guys from my old unit. But geez, I hope no one was as close to the mortars as us."

I'm breathing deeply into my diaphragm, my adrenaline is still pumping. I have never felt anything like this. I've just run faster than I've ever run before, faster than on my first day here. I was within yards of mortars going off. Shrapnel was probably shooting all around me. I could have almost died or been wounded, yet it was a rush. The only difference is that I don't want an award.

Actually, I'm amazed and sickened; they seem unaware or don't care how close we just came to death. At this moment, I vow to never receive any ribbons. Why would I need an award for surviving an attack? If that's the case, all the survivors should get one. Is that a good word to call veterans, merely *survivors*?

WEEK 4, DAY 4, IRAQ

0730 HOURS, OR

I'm in a better mood than I've been in for a while. I feel rambunctious and a little mischievous, and I decide to pull a prank. My target is Hudge because she's having the toughest time right now. The plan is that Crade, who has also been looking a little downtrodden lately due to problems he's experiencing with his soon to be baby's mother—anyway, I don't want to go into it here; he's going to help me.

1430 HOURS, OR

While I finish up my last surgery, Crade is informing everyone else of our plan. The thought of an overweight Satanist on tiptoes whispering into everyone's ears, with all his BO after a shift, is cracking me up.

1500 HOURS, OR

I'm scrubbed in for surgery and we're about to begin a fasciotomy, a procedure to relieve pressure in the muscle or tissue, on the left leg of a patient. Since this wound is on the left leg, during surgery the only thing showing is the leg; everything else is covered with sterile sheets. I tell Reto to have Hudge scrub me out and take over my surgery so I can go home for the day. Immediately the doctor starts yelling at her, asking what took her so long to get scrubbed in. Giving him a look that says "Fuck off," Hudge changes positions with me, and I hand the case over to her. As I'm telling her where all the instruments are—and what to expect for the case—the patient starts convulsing badly, his entire body shaking under the sheets.

The doctor looks at Hudge.

"Grab his legs; hold him down so that he doesn't fall off of the bed."

The patient moans from beneath the blanket. His face is covered but we all hear it.

The doctor turns toward the anesthesiologist. "What the hell did you give him? He's still awake—get him sedated."

Hudge grabs the patient's leg as best she can while still staying sterile.

The anesthesiologist pushes a few buttons and the patient stops shaking. The room is silent for a second. The doctor asks for a scalpel; Hudge hands him one.

Again, the patient starts convulsing. Hudge grabs the patient by the legs.

"I thought I told you to hold him down," the doctor screams.

The doctor is yelling at the anesthesiologist: "I told you to sedate him. Shoot him full of something." He tells Hudge to grab the legs tighter. The patient is shaking so badly he might fall. Hudge leans on the legs with all of her weight and grips them tight. The doctor tells her to move her grip up further on the patient to hold his waist down.

"AAARRRRGGGGHH," the patient yells as he sits up in the bed and grabs Hudge by the waist. Hudge screams. She jumps back and hits the instrument table. I can tell she is scared. Her chest is heaving. She's looks around at everyone and no one is doing anything. She looks at the patient uncovered on the table, it's Crade, who is laughing an evil Satanic laugh.

Hudge rips off her mask and gown and throws it to the ground.

"Oh. My. God. You assholes!"

WEEK 4, DAY 5, IRAQ

0730 HOURS, OR

Captain Cardine is the hospital commander. She's stout with a dark skin tone and perfectly white teeth. When she smiles it can be seen for miles. I have no idea why I actually have to go to her office—Gagney wouldn't tell me. Like most people probably would, I immediately assume I'm in some type of trouble. When I walk in the door, I know it's good news, though, or at least not bad news. Captain Cardine tells me that she heard I was on guard duty the day of the recent mortar attack and I'm qualified for a Combat Action Badge (CAB) for being in a combat situation. All I have to do is fill out some paperwork, tell the story of what happened, and verify it with the other two soldiers, Elwood and Boredo. I remember the vow I made in the bunker.

"Ma'am. With all due respect, I would not like any awards."

Captain Cardine looks at me a little confused.

"What do you mean, you wouldn't like an award? You're going to be one of the first in the unit to be awarded the CAB."

"I understand Ma'am, it's just that . . . all I did was run to a bunker. I was following orders."

Captain Cardine stares at me.

"Soldier, I'm not sure if we're on the same page here. This isn't a big deal, just fill out the paperwork so that we can give you the award."

I look at Captain Cardine, and it is clear that we're not on the same page. I try to explain my feelings to her again, but she doesn't . . . she can't understand why anyone wouldn't want an award. Captain Cardine slides the paper toward me.

"Soldier, I don't think you understand. I want you to fill out this paperwork. I want you to get that award. It not only looks

good on you to get the award, but it looks good on us as a unit
to give the award. Besides, Elwood and Boredo already filled out
their paperwork. They came to me the next morning. They were
excited and they can't get the awards if you don't fill out the paperwork. To get the award you need at least two witnesses not including yourself. They need you to verify their stories. I don't know
what the big deal is, soldier, just fill out the paperwork."

I leave her office having signed the paperwork and written my
story. I find Reto and tell him I just sold my soul.

WEEK 4, DAY 6, IRAQ

0440 HOURS, MY ROOM

I don't know if it's because of the last mortar attack and that
being fearful for my death has given me new energy, but I wake
up very early today. It's so early, it's still dark outside. It's that
type of dark where the moon is gone from the sky and the sun
isn't visible yet, but you can tell it will be shortly. When I usually
wake up, I take a right down the road toward the dining facility,
gym, and the Hajji stores. Today I decide to take a left. There
are empty buildings, a fence, a dry cleaners, sleeping barracks for
another unit, and sand everywhere. I keep walking, and down
the road I see a red pickup truck idling at a stop sign. There's
someone sitting inside the truck. He works for KBR, civilian
contractors the Army hired to do odds jobs on base. There was no
reason for anyone to be out—unless you're going for a morning
walk. The chow hall doesn't open for breakfast for another hour,

the Hajji stores also don't open for a few hours, and shift change isn't until 0700.

I am in the shadows of the street as I walk. There are no streetlights near me, but there is one directly above the pickup truck. My suspicion of all things odd, or I suppose voyeurism, gets a hold of me, and I duck behind a tree to see what's going on. The windows are dark and the truck is tall. The man is looking off into space. The truck just idles at the stop sign. The man in the truck and I are the only ones awake on the entire base, I bet. He's staring straight ahead, enjoying the silence. I notice that the light from the street lamp casts a small shadow into the truck, and the shadow inside the truck is bobbing: up, down, up, down, up, down. I see a head at the man's waist. It appears for a second and goes back down.

A damn cat's rustling the garbage. I turn around—the noise came from behind me. Then I look back. Captain Tarr's getting out of the truck. She looks both ways across the road to make sure no one sees her. She starts walking briskly back toward the sleeping area; I know she doesn't see me. The truck speeds off and I continue to stand there.

If this is what has gotten her to lighten her mood and stop yelling at everyone, then I don't care if she's breaking the rules. I tell myself I should run after the truck and tell the guy to keep up the good work.

I walk to the area where the old dining facility used to be. It's still dark, and when I get to the building I see that there are bright green lights surrounding it. Glow sticks. Reto and I had seen the same kind two nights before. We thought it was strange but we didn't say anything at the time. Now that I think about it, the night after we saw those lights, the area near the building got hit bad with mortars. Maybe our base has been infiltrated and there are spies placing the glow sticks around so the enemy combatants know where to aim. Nah, never mind. If that were the case someone else would have noticed by now. Still, I'm gonna tell Gagney—just in case.

0700 HOURS, OR

"Anthony," Gagney is telling me, "Captain Cardine wants you to go to her office again. You better not be in fucking trouble. If you make me look bad, so help me God. . . ." Gagney trails off.

"Before I go I wanted to tell you that I saw these glow sticks around the old dining facility, and Reto and I had seen them two nights before and then the building in the area got hit with mortars and. . . ."

Gagney is walking away; he's not listening. He never listens, but there's nothing I can do about it, and besides, I'm sure I'm just being paranoid about the green glow sticks. I turn around and head toward Captain Cardine's office. Again, I assume that I'm in trouble, but the fear abates when I see her and she's smiling. She tells me that the CABs for the other two soldiers have been approved. Mine, however, has been denied.

"Michael . . ." Captain Cardine says, using my first name as if we're now pals. "When Elwood and Boredo wrote their stories, only Elwood said you were there. Boredo never mentioned you in his story." Just like Boredo, I think to myself. "Since Boredo didn't mention you, you won't be getting the award."

My mind spins. Boredo wants only him and Elwood to get the awards. No matter what, I need to make sure I get this award, if only to rub it in Boredo's face. I've already sold my soul by signing the paperwork; now, it's as if I'm not getting paid. I know this is childish and pointless, but I'm in Iraq, what else is there to do?

"Well, I was there, ma'am. Tell me what I need to do so that I can get that award."

"I didn't think you wanted it."

"I just want to help my unit look good. I mean the more awards we hand out, the better you and everyone else looks, right?"

Captain Cardine smiles.

"That's right, soldier, glad to see you're aboard. Find Boredo, tell him to include you in his story."

After leaving Cardine, I find Boredo. I tell him I'll recant my story unless he includes me in his. He looks at me and frowns as if I have just told him I am the devil and I want his firstborn son, but he's not stupid. He grabs his coat and storms off toward Captain Cardine's office.

1045 HOURS, HOSPITAL

He looks bad. An Iraqi patient. Machines to his left are breathing for him, raising his chest up and down. To his right is a pole with different liquids being fed into his veins. On his leg is a bag attached to a catheter in his penis; all of the liquids being fed into his veins come right out into the bag. He's brain dead and now merely serves as a vessel for the liquid to go from one container to the next. The doctors shine light into his eyes, and his pupils give no reaction. They hit him in the face with their hands and on the knees with their reflex hammers—no reaction, no nervous system, nothing.

We are a small hospital with limited resources. We get several new patients every day and we can't afford to keep them here that long. Often we have to ship the American patients to Germany or Texas, and we send the Iraqis to local Iraqi hospitals. The severely injured go to American hospitals either in different parts of Iraq, Germany, or back in the States. We only do this for Iraqis that have been hurt by us.

Everyone is gathered around the Iraqi. I know what they are all thinking and what decision is being debated.

When is a person really dead? When the heart is no longer beating? Or how about when the brain stops? This man is lying in a hospital bed, machines breathe for him, his right arm has a tube in it sending liquid into him, and through his penile shaft there is another tube draining the same fluid right back out. As long as the body is being fed oxygen, the heart will continue to beat and give the impression that the body is alive. The brain, however, is gone; there's no coming back.

We didn't injure him and we don't have the supplies, equipment, or the interest to send him to one of our stateside hospitals where he'll just exist for a few more moments, eventually die, and cost the taxpayers a million dollars in the process. The Iraqi hospitals don't have the equipment or supplies to take care of him. One of the doctors makes a decision and talks to a member of the Iraqi's family. He walks over to the machine and pulls the plug. The family member weeps; a small crowd gathers around; the chaplain is called. Some of the other patients that are close by bow their heads in solace. The patient's chest goes up one last time and then goes back down for its final breath; the man is officially dead, in mind, spirit, and now body.

I watch for a moment then turn and head back to the OR.

WEEK 4, DAY 7, IRAQ

0300 HOURS, MY ROOM

BOOMMM! BOOMMM! BAANNGG!
"Bunkers! Bunkers! Bunkers!"

I open my eyes as I lay in bed. I can hear mortars hitting the base and the loudspeaker yelling—we are under attack again. A few hours ago I took four sleeping pills to fall asleep, and now I'm supposed to wake up and run to a bunker. I know I need to get out of bed but I can't. I can't move my legs, or maybe it's just that I don't want to move my legs.

BBOOOMMM!!

Another mortar hits. I either don't want to get out of bed bad enough or I literally can't because of the sleeping pills—either way my legs don't move. They're so loud, the mortars. They're hitting the old dining facility and the area around it—I'm too tired or in a daze to care. I look over at Markham. He's getting out of bed and heading toward the bunker.

"Markham," I yell, using all my might. "Come and get me when the attack is over, so I can be accounted for." Markham nods and leaves. In the night not everyone makes it to the bunkers. They're extremely cold and many people opt for sleep in their own warm bed, despite the obvious risk.

MONTH 3

"IT'S THE SILENCE THAT DRIVES US MAD."

WEEK 1, DAY 1, IRAQ

0800 HOURS, OR

When I first heard that Sergeant Waters's boyfriend was coming to our hospital as an ICU nurse I was determined not to like him. Then just a few minutes ago I met him—Staff Sergeant McClee. He jokes around with me and Reto; he fits right in. He's an unassuming 5'6", 160 lbs., red hair and freckles. The spitting image of an old Irish boy. Don't get me wrong. I'm sure Waters filled his head with pre-existing prejudices, just as our heads are filled with pre-existing prejudices of anyone who would go out with Waters; but I like him. He's filling in paperwork now and is going to take a few classes to get himself acquainted with our hospital, find out the way we do things.

2000 HOURS, AUDITORIUM

"And this is why I will be going away on leave, soldiers. I don't want to leave ya'll behind, but I have family business I need to take care of." Command Sergeant Major Ridge—the leader for the entire enlisted section, the man who got drunk in Iraq and threatened to send his sergeants to the frontline if they complain—is giving a speech to all of the enlisted soldiers. I'm not sure what it's about yet, but Ridge seems emotional and sober so it must be important.

"I will be taking leave because, like many of you, I have family issues going on back home. My son has just tried to commit suicide." A hush falls over everyone in the audience. Even the people who don't like Command Sergeant Major Ridge are quiet. "Thank God his attempt wasn't successful, but I've talked to

Colonel Tucker and we both feel that I should take some time off and fly home to be with my son and help him through this ordeal. I want you all to know that I will be thinking about you while I am gone. I think of you all as my sons and daughters and I will miss you, but for a few weeks I need to be with my family during this hour of need."

I can't help but feel, as I walk out of the auditorium, that with all of Ridge's faults and even being the lackey of Colonel Tucker (actually everyone refers to him as Colonel Jelly because a two-star general once called him a spineless asshole), he is still only a human trying to survive in the world.

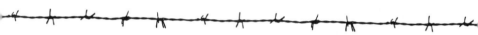

WEEK 1, DAY 6, IRAQ

2000 HOURS, OR

"I don't give a shit what he has. When he's in my OR, I make the rules. I'm not going to treat anyone special just because they are 'special,' says Dr. John, one of the surgeons from the FST.

"Well, back home I work with children with autism and there's a certain way you have to deal with them," says Captain Tarr.

They are fighting over Lieutenant Quinn, a 6'4" Caucasian man. His jet-black hair and squinty eyes make him look like he could be a tall Asian man. He also, according to Captain Tarr, has undiagnosed Asperger's, which is a mild form of autism.

"This is bullshit. If he does have Asperger's, then how the fuck did he even get into the Army? And besides, that doesn't excuse him from screwing up my surgery and almost getting a patient killed," John yells back.

Captain Tarr doesn't want to have this argument, but she knows she's already in too deep. She can't back down now.

"Listen, it's something to be dealt with. I've had family members with this problem. He's just having trouble adjusting to the change of atmosphere."

Chandler walks in just in time to hear them yelling. "What are those two fighting about?"

I look over at Chandler and the Pepsi in his hand. He drinks so much, he now only has a few teeth left.

"They're yelling about Quinn screwing up a case."

Chandler laughs. Lieutenant Quinn has been acting strange lately. The type of strange where if you asked him why he was rubbing honey all over his body he'd reply with, "Oh . . . I thought it was vinegar." On a good day you avoid him; on a bad day Colonel Reke would send him home telling him to take the day off. The last nurse is Colonel Reke. She is in charge of the nurses for the OR, as well as Staff Sergeant Gagney. She is in her late fifties and still has golden blond hair. With her tiny figure and rosy red lipstick, she also reminds me of my grandmother. She is a former Special Forces nurse and CEO of a hospital. She never seems to be around. It's as if she's always doing something else besides being in the OR.

"I was the scrub tech and Lieutenant Quinn was my nurse for the case," I say to Chandler.

"When the surgery started, Quinn was nowhere to be found. Twenty minutes into the surgery, he walks in the room. Then he leaves again and ten minutes later he comes back in and starts mopping the floor—while our surgery is still going on! Dr. John then started yelling at him saying, 'You can't mop during surgery! You'll kick dirt into the air. Get the hell out of here!'

"Lieutenant Quinn stares back at him and walks out of the room like a little kid that's been told no more cookies before dinner. Quinn then walks back in and stares at the doctor, just stands there—staring. John doesn't notice and asks him for some saline, and then, out of nowhere, Quinn starts freaking out:

'What kind of saline? Do you want normal saline? What percentage sodium? What size bag . . . large, medium, small? I need to know these things before I leave the room or else I'll be walking back and forth, back and forth, back and forth. Or is that what you want, you want me to go back and forth, back and forth, just for your . . . amusement . . . huh, is that it. . . ?'

'The one we always use,' John yells, and he goes back to focusing on the patient.

"Next John asks for suture and Quinn lists every type of suture we have. Quinn does the same thing every time the doctor asks for something, so eventually Johns starts to make do with what he has. Out of the corner of my eye I see Quinn fooling around with the bovie machine. I don't say anything because I don't want him freaking out on me. Captain Tarr then comes in to relieve Quinn so that he can go get some lunch.

'Bovie,' John yells at me to hand it to him.

'Why the hell isn't this working?' John yells when the bovie doesn't turn on.

"The patient is now bleeding profusely and we can't stop the bleeding because the bovie machine—which is used to cauterize—isn't working.

'Mosquito clamp and suture,' John yells out at me, as we clamp off the blood vessel and tie it off to stop the bleeding, giving us time to find out what's wrong.

"Tarr starts frantically pushing buttons on the machine. Then she says, 'Someone unplugged the machine and the switches are in the opposite direction.'

'This is bullshit,' Dr. John screams, throwing a pair of scissors to the ground. I hand him the bovie tip and he cauterizes the skin. The surgery ends and John rushes off, saying that he's got some business to take care of and he tells me to finish up. John finds Colonel Reke, tells her what happened, and Reke tells Quinn to go home for the day."

"John wants Lieutenant Quinn kicked out of the military."

WEEK 2, DAY 1, IRAQ

2000 HOURS, AUDITORIUM

Four women from my unit had decided to dress up in sexy lingerie and sing "Lady Marmalade" in a talent show. If I didn't know them, I guess I'd say they were sexy; the only problem is that I do know them, and they've been sleeping around ever since they got to Iraq. The men in the audience all clapped, smiled, and yelled to the ladies. The women in the audience shook their heads in disapproval. The flier for the show clearly says: "Be warned, explicit content."

The next day one of the women in the audience—an old woman who probably hasn't had sex in ten years—complains that the evening was too provocative. She said she saw a poster for the show and read the warning that it might be a little graphic and adult oriented. But she never thought that it'd be anything like that. Now we're not allowed to have any more shows like that.

Six thousand miles away from home and our only entertainment is gossip and the occasional PG-rated show we put on in the theater.

WEEK 2, DAY 5, IRAQ

0700 HOURS, OR

"So do you want the bad story or the worst story?" Denti asks as I place my breakfast tray on the OR break room table. I have discovered that since surgeries don't start until 0800 and I normally have to wait from 0700 to 0800 for the doctors, instead of waking up at 0600 to eat, I can wake up at 0630—a half-hour later than I was previously—and eat at the OR. The downside is I have to listen to Denti talk as I eat—or as he steals a bagel off my plate.

"You want to hear the worst or the most perverted—well, actually, they're both kind of perverted."

"It's too early to talk—"

"Just listen to me. You know about two weeks ago Sergeant Major Ridge gave that speech about going home to be with his suicidal son?"

Denti doesn't wait for me to reply.

"Well, he went home on a plane with a bunch of other people who were going on leave. One of those people was Sergeant Henderson."

Sergeant Henderson is a medic with our southern hospital.

"Henderson and Ridge both get back to the States and take the same plane back since they're from the same town. Henderson is home for a few days and decides to go out to a bar and play some pool with his buddies. And he's bent over a pool table shooting when he overhears one of his friends say:

"'Check out this old guy grabbing that girl's ass.'

Henderson looks up—

"'Oh my God. That's the command sergeant major for my unit.'

Ridge takes several girls to a private booth in the back of the pool hall.

"'Just let the old man have some fun,' Henderson's friend yells to him.

"'He's got a daughter the same ages as these girls, too.' Henderson says back."

Denti pauses to take a piece of bacon from my plate; he pisses me off.

"As I was saying," he starts back up again.

"Why don't you get your own bacon?"

"Listen, listen, listen." He's already eating it. "What happened was Henderson goes back to playing pool and sees Ridge leave the bar with two prostitutes."

"Some time of need for his family, what a dickhead, I can't believe I felt bad for him."

"That's not even the perverted one," Denti says. "You know the education courses? Since Waters's boyfriend is new here he's taking his education classes."

I roll my eyes at Denti at the mere mention of Colonel Lessly, the man who's in charge of the education classes. He got in trouble before we even got deployed. Colonel Lessly was put on special orders to be on active duty before we got deployed and was in charge of getting our unit's inventory ready. He looks like the biker from the Village People, but in an Army uniform. Specialist Wilson also got put on orders early. Wilson is a twenty-eight-year-old man who is about sixty pounds overweight—with all of it in his gut. He's not the sharpest tool in the shed. If you ask him what time it is, he'll stare at you for fifteen seconds, his watch for twenty, stare at you again for fifteen seconds and then tell you the wrong time.

"One night Lessly invites Wilson to dinner and a movie. They went out on a Friday night. Over the next few days Wilson got three e-mails from Lessly. The first one asks him if he had fun at the movies, and Lessly attaches a picture of two animals having sex and a caption that says: 'Doesn't that look fun?' In the next e-mail there's a picture of a monkey eating a banana shaped like a penis, and the caption says: 'The things I could do to that banana.' Wilson doesn't answer the e-mails. I don't think it even occurred to him how weird this was. On Sunday Wilson receives another e-mail. Colonel Lessly asks Wilson if he can 'suck his dick.' Wilson freaks out. He prints the e-mails and shows them to Mardine. She shows them to the GOBs, and you know what they told Lessly to do? You ready for this? 'Don't talk to Wilson anymore.'"

✠

"HEY. If you want to hear the story, pay attention." I hear Denti say, taking me out of my daze. "Oh shit, Anthony, you never listen—the point is that Colonel Lessly is now making the moves on McClee—"

✠

BAAAANNNGGG. BAAAAANNNNGGG.
BUNKERS! BUNKERS! BUNKERS!

1500 HOURS, OR

Our surgeries are out early today after we each did three I&Ds.
When Reto walks in for second shift he's got a paper with him.
"What patient died in the OR?" he asks. Denti and I look up.

"None."

No patient has died in the OR. Patients of ours have died at
later dates, but up to this time no patient has died in our OR—as
far as I'm aware.

"Let me see that."

We go over to see this.

Denti says, "What are you talking about? This is wrong. What
is this, yellow journalism?"

"Probably some mistake."

"No patients have died in the OR."

"An American soldier died on the operating table," Reto is
reading.

"That's not true. No patient died, not in the OR, I remember
that surgery. There was an American soldier and Iraqi. Now, yes,
the patient in question did end up dying, but he died later in the
ICW. But the patient was alive, he didn't die during surgery here
in the OR. . . . "

We have an advanced copy of the article written by the journalists who visited the OR a few months ago. The article is a pow-
der puff piece about our unit and it blatantly lies about a patient
dying in the OR—the journalists were in there when we wheeled
the patient out alive.

We're all just standing there in silence.

WEEK 2, DAY 6, IRAQ

2330 HOURS, MY ROOM

I normally go to sleep at 2200 hours, ten o'clock, but I can't sleep anymore. I've been taking sleeping pills almost every night. The pills are still working, but I have to take more and more each night to fall asleep.

I spend a half-hour tossing and turning in bed and decide to go outside and smoke a cigarette.

"Anthony, what's up, man?" I turn and see Specialist Steve. Steve is a friend of mine from the unit. Tall, gangly, white as a ghost.

"I thought you were down south."

"Not me."

"Working?"

"You just getting off?"

"Yeah, man, been working night shift ever since we got here. Twelve hours on, twelve hours off, sleep. Twelve hours on, twelve hours off, sleep."

"That's what I'm trying to do right now myself—go to sleep. Pills aren't working."

"NyQuil, man. I've been using it for a couple weeks. Down a couple of shots before bed and you sleep twelve hours."

✚

I make a note to buy NyQuil.

WEEK 3, DAY 1, IRAQ

0145 HOURS, MY ROOM

Earlier in the day I go to the store to buy some NyQuil, but it was sold out. The sales clerk tells me nighttime medicines sell out the second they come in, and he won't have another shipment in for two weeks. If I really want the NyQuil, though, I should check back every day in case they get the shipment early. He tells me that there's a tall, skinny, white man named Steve who comes in every other day looking for NyQuil and I should do what he does.

I have four sleeping pills in me and I still can't sleep. I've smoked two cigarettes and my mind is on fire.

As I lay here I am beginning to notice all the different noises in Iraq.

Bang!

I hear a loud noise; it's a dumpster hitting the ground but it sounds like a mortar. Both noises sound similar, but it takes a trained ear to differentiate the two. Sometimes you hear a loud noise and cannot tell whether it is the beginning of a mortar attack and you should grab your weapon or whether it is a dumpster hitting the ground and you should go back to sleep.

There's a string of gunfire heard in the background, but I can't tell if the guns are being fired to kill or as practice. Every noise has a different nuance and every sound has a different meaning.

I think of the Buddha. What is the sound of one hand clapping. . . ? If a tree falls in the forest, but no one. . . ? If a bullet rips through the body of a terrorist, splitting his skin and bones to fragments, but no one. . . ? I know now what people mean when they say, "A shot heard around the world."

But as terrifying as the noises and sounds might be, nothing compares to the silences, the silence as I lay here in bed. Silence is the real killer. It leaves you no other devices but your own thoughts, and when you are fighting a war your thoughts aren't too often good. There are many types of silences. The silence of fatigue after a long day in the OR. The silence of doubt after twelve hours of surgery when the patient still dies. The silence of fear just after a mortar attack. My mind races. Is it a mortar or a dumpster? Should I get out of bed or stay in bed? Do I even care if I die? Is someone now dying? Is someone now dead? Am I dead?

Silence. . . . I hear the dump truck drive away. I need to go back to sleep. It's the silence that drives us mad. That drives us to commit suicide or cheat on our wives or ruin someone's life.

It's the silence that kills us.

WEEK 3, DAY 2, IRAQ

0215 HOURS, MY ROOM

BBBBAAAAMMMMMMMMMMMM!!!
I sit up straight in bed.
BBBBAAAAMMMMMMMMMMMM!!!
BBBBAAAAMMMMMMMMMMMM!!!
BBBBOOOOOOOOOOOMMMMM!!!
BUNKERS. BUNKERS. BUNKERS.

It's an attack and the rounds are hitting close. I look at my clock; it says 2:15. I look over on my nightstand at the half-empty bottle of Nyquil. I know I should get out of bed but I don't feel like moving.

BBBBAAAAMMMMMMMMMMM!!!

The rounds are really close. I don't think I've heard them this close, hitting inside our barracks.

I know I should get out of bed; they're hitting inside our sleeping compound. I look back at the clock: 2:17. I look at the half-empty bottle of NyQuil that Steve finally gave me. I look at the inside of my eyelids.

BBBBBBBBBAAAAAAAAAAMMMMMMMMMMMM!!!!!!!!!

2:20. I know I need to get up. I look over at Markham to see if he's out of bed. He's gone and our door is wide open.

BBBBBBBBBAAAAAAAAAAMMMMMMMMMMMM!!!!!!!!!

I know I've got to move fast, so I grab my weapon and head to the closest bunker, which luckily is only a few feet away. My heart is pounding but I'm not sure if it's from the rush or the NyQuil. I run to the bunker. By the time I get there everyone from my street is already there—*BBBBBBBBBBBBAAAAAAAAAAAAAMMM-MMMMMMMMMMM!!!!!!!!!*

BBBBBBBBBBBBAAAAAAAAAAAAAMMMMMMMMMM-MMMMM!!!!!!!!!

BBBBBBBBOOOOOOOOOOOOOOOOOOOMMMMMMM-MMMMM!!!!!!!!!

CCCRRRAAAAASSSSSHHH!!!!

Everyone in the bunker looks at one another; those last two hits sounded like they hit someone's room. It's freezing outside. It's the beginning of winter. I'm only wearing a T-shirt and shorts. It is almost Christmas.

0325 HOURS, BUNKER

It takes over an hour for the bombings to stop and the base to be all cleared again. Because it's a few blocks closer to our rooms than the hospital, Gagney lets us check in at his room.

✚

On my way back I see a huge crowd of people gathered around a Chu (sleeping quarter) that's on the street after mine. Everyone is crowded around Sergeant Elster's room.

Sergeant Mardine comes through the crowd telling everyone to back up a hundred feet.

"There is an unexploded mortar on the ground."

Elster sees me and makes his way through the crowd.

"What the hell happened?" I ask.

"Man, I'll tell you, Anthony, that was crazy. When the second one hit I got up and the next one went through the room. It went through my damn wall!"

✚

The mortars are directly hitting our sleeping barracks now. Before I couldn't sleep because of the fear of being mortared, but now it's not even a fear, it's a reality.

WEEK 3, DAY 3, IRAQ

1100 HOURS, HOSPITAL

'Twas the night before Christmas and all through the world, not a creature was stirring . . . except in Iraq.

✚

Elster is in the back part of the hospital and looking in big military shipping containers—one of the supply conexes—and doing inventory of what he has and needs to order.

"Gagney wants you to come inside; he's having a meeting."

"Gagney just told me to come out here ten minutes ago," Elster yells from inside the conex.

"Whatever, man, that's what he told me."

Elster comes out of the conex and we go back toward the front of the hospital. We're clearing our weapons—

BBBBBAAAAAAAMMMMM!!!

BBBBBAAAAAAAMMMMM!!!

BUNKERS. BUNKERS. BUNKERS.

Ninety percent of the mortars are hitting directly on top of the hospital, which is reinforced with two feet of cement. It starts exploding again:

BAAMMM . . . BBBBAAAAMMMM . . .

Some people, like Reto, seem to get used to working through it.

BAAAAAMMMM!

When I help Elster finish the supply inventory later, three people are staring at the ground where we were talking about Gagney at the conex.

Two mortars hit right there.

Elster and I examine the ground. There's a hole the size of a football. One of the guys that was standing around takes out a camera and begins taking pictures of the other conexes in the area. They're made of solid steel, and now, from the mortar, they have shrapnel peppered throughout them.

Both of us are thinking the same thing. Two times in a row, incredibly close calls, saved by only seconds. Maybe he's not so lucky.

1145 HOURS, HOSPITAL

This is what Reto knows about the hospital roof:

"Like two seconds ago I went to the roof of the hospital to check out what type of damage had happened. And it was hit pretty bad, all kind of indents everywhere. That's what I was expecting to find, but do you want to know what else I found? The whole roof, littered with condoms and condom wrappers. It looks like there was literally an orgy up there."

A few nights ago Crade was telling me how he took his girlfriend to the roof of the hospital to look at the stars.

WEEK 3, DAY 4, IRAQ

1100 HOURS, OR

Christmas. We do a secret Santa. I don't get the warm pajamas I wanted; instead I get a VHS movie called *Air Bud*. Just what I wanted: an old movie about a dog that plays basketball, and best of all it's in Spanish. I think the person who gave it to me must have confused me with Torres, but I laugh it off and put a fake smile on my face.

Everyone hands out presents and tries to have a good time, but really we're all just depressed and miss our families. It's Christmas but it doesn't mean anything. We're still thousands of miles away from our families and in the middle of a war.

In the end we spend the rest of the day doing as little that's memorable as possible. No one wants to be able to remember Christmas in Iraq. All we want is to pass the day as quickly as any other. We want to chalk it off on the calendars so that we can say one more day has gone by that we won't remember and we are one day closer to being back with our families.

WEEK 4, DAY 4, IRAQ

2300 HOURS, MY ROOM

In all the war movies I've ever seen, no one calls home or goes on MySpace. They write emotional letters, and even though I can't do the emotional part, I still send the letters. I've heard from about half the people I've written.

I read stories about friends celebrating their twenty-first birthdays, twenty-one shots in twenty-one bars, the typical crazy animal house college stories—the drama, this guy, and this girl, who's doing what and with whom. It just depresses the hell out of me. I remember watching movies about people growing up, going to college, meeting girls, having a great time, and becoming mature adults. My friends that do write tell stories of going to bars and drinking all night. I spent that same night working a twenty-four-hour shift. I read stories of one-night stands and empty hookups. I spent that night operating on someone only to have them die the next day in the ICW. I read stories of friends going to concerts and frat parties. I spent that night cowering in a bunker for my life. I should be home with my friends. This isn't how a twenty-year-old should be spending his glory years. When I graduated high school the keynote speaker told us the next few years would be the best years of our lives. Yet here I am, six thousand miles from home and fighting a war. Of course, I don't regret my choice. But only when my tour's over will I find out if it was the right one.

I don't want to write any more letters and I don't want to receive any more, but if I don't write back, friends and family will write just to see if I'm okay. So I have to write back, and it turns into a never-ending cycle.

Soon the letters from the third and fourth graders will start to come. Those are the most depressing of them all. Kids writing letters supporting something they know nothing about, only that they're told to support their country and the war. Some kids will draw pictures of the American flag and men in uniform and send them to us. Every now and again we'll get cards and letters from a kid whose parent died in the war; those are the most difficult to read, and you know you've got to reply to them. The worst story I ever heard was about a little kid whose father died during the first invasion of Iraq. A few years went by and the kid learned how to read and write, so he sent letters to some of the soldiers in Iraq. One of the soldiers with kids of his own felt bad and wrote back, so they became pen pals. A few months later that soldier died, but the kid kept writing. Another soldier in the unit didn't know what to do with the letters. He knew the guy had been writing to the kid but the kid didn't know he was dead, so that soldier became the kid's penpal, but he got killed, too. I hope that the kid doesn't start writing to me. He's bad fucking luck. I'm depressed just thinking about it.

✚

Happy New Year.

MONTH 4

"HOW ARE WE
SUPPOSED
TO SPOT THE
REAL SUICIDAL
PEOPLE WHEN
EVERYONE
HAS SUICIDAL
SYMPTOMS?"

WEEK 1, DAY 1, IRAQ

0700 HOURS, HOSPITAL

Well, it's official: There has been a rumor going around for a few weeks now, but it's finally confirmed. We are moving bases. Our new base will be in the western part of Iraq in the Anbar province. A new hospital is being built on a Marine base, and they need someone to run it. There is already a Navy hospital there, but they aren't doing well enough to run a new hospital. Here, a stateside active duty Army unit will be coming in to replace us, and we will move southwest to the Al Anbar province of Iraq to our new hospital.

I guess you could say it was a compliment to us since they approached us about the job.

But since they did, we have to inventory our entire hospital and its entire contents, from a pair of disposable surgical gloves to heart rate monitors to tongue depressors and ventilators. Everything needs to be inventoried and then inventoried again and then again. The move date is not set in stone and the new hospital isn't even built. It is expected to take a month or two to build.

WEEK 1, DAY 3, IRAQ

0700 HOURS, OR

The Army explained to us very clearly that while in Iraq no one is allowed to have sex. Of course, this doesn't stop anyone, but our unit is trying to enforce it. We are the military—all adults—fighting a war, and men and women are not allowed to be in the same sleeping area. A woman can't set foot in a man's room and vice versa. This is why people are having sex on the roof of the hospital.

I walk into work and Crade is in back eating breakfast. His head is down. A few weeks ago he told me that before we left for Iraq he had gotten a woman pregnant. A few days ago he told me the woman is threatening to never let him see his baby. I don't say anything to him.

"Guys . . . this is the best, this one is absolutely crazy. . . ."

I turn from Crade and stare at Denti.

"What? What are you talking about?"

"Check this out . . ." Denti says as he reaches over and takes a piece of bacon from Crade's plate. Crade throws his fork down and walks out of the room. Crade's mood is transparent, and I know I should probably follow him and see what's wrong.

"You know Specialist Porpe and Specialist Meade, right?" Denti begins.

I nod at Denti; of course I know the two girls he's talking about.

"Sergeant Smith caught them having an orgy in their room with two guys from supply."

"Will you shut up, Denti?"

"You know she's the lesbian lover of First Sergeant Mardine."

"Just shut up, okay?"

WEEK 1, DAY 5, IRAQ

0700 HOURS, OR

I will say it once again: Gagney is a smarter man than we give him credit for. He knows we would have all complained about his bad attitude and manipulation of Hudge, so he conveniently forgets to tell us that there was a climate control meeting. It was our one opportunity to truly tell the leadership what's going on and how he treats us, but ironically, Gagney was the one who was supposed to tell us when the meeting was—and now it's too late. I don't know how he does it, but it's like he's always one step ahead. There is literally nothing we can do about him because the one chance we would have had to complain about him, he didn't tell us about—and now we can't even complain about that. To be honest, I'm not surprised by anything Gagney does; he is either a diabolical genius, or a nitwit.

WEEK 2, DAY 1, IRAQ

0700 HOURS, OR

During one of the suicide briefings that the Army gives us, they mention a statistic that says the majority of people who talk about suicide don't usually attempt it; it's just a cry for help.

I always wondered about that statistic, though, because if that's the case, then the ones who do talk about suicide are the only ones we know who won't kill themselves, and it's everyone else that's a possibility.

In that same suicide briefing they also tell us that people who are suicidal usually become depressed from big changes happening in their lives. They say that depressed people become withdrawn and will not enjoy everyday activities. They'll sleep a lot.

I couldn't help but laugh when I heard this at the suicide prevention class, because I looked around the room and everyone fit the criteria. We've all had a huge change in our lives coming to Iraq. Everyone here is withdrawn and sleeps as much as possible, and our everyday activities consist of running for our lives and working on near-death patients. Who wouldn't be depressed and want to spend time alone? We work long hours at unpredictable times, and we see the same people twenty-four hours a day, seven days a week. What I never understood from these classes is how are we supposed to spot the real suicidal people when everyone has suicidal symptoms?

✚

Denti's head is low and he doesn't grab any bacon off of my plate as I put it down. "What's the matter with you?" I ask putting my tray down, still protecting my bacon.

Denti looks up.

"Crade tried to kill himself."

"Crade?"

"Yeah."

"Jesus. How?"

"Dust-Off."

✚

There have been several reported deaths in the United States about kids dying from Dust-Off (it's the stuff you clean your keyboard with). The gas that gets you high in Dust-Off is called R2. It's used in refrigeration. It's a heavy gas that weighs more than air, which means as you inhale it; the gas pushes all your oxygenated air out. It's similar to doing whip-its. It gives people a dizzy, light-headed feeling, and it's why kids use it to get high. But it also decreases oxygen to your heart and your head, and it can kill you. When you use it, you don't suddenly do too much and overdose. Death can happen in one hit. There are reports and stories of kids dying with their eyes open and the Dust-Off straw still in their mouths.

"Maybe he was just trying to get high," I say to Denti after a few minutes of awkward silence.

"He was a heavy partier, maybe he was just looking for a quick high. I mean if he wanted to kill himself we have weapons with hundreds of rounds. It would only take one shot."

My answer seems to perk Denti up for the moment; the possibility that it could have been just an attempt to get high lightens both our moods. But in the back of my mind I can't help but think of the possible events that led up to this: Crade reading the Satanic bible, acting distant the past few days. . . .

I chose to listen to Denti's story the other day rather than go ask Crade how he was feeling.

Maybe this is my fault?

WEEK 2, DAY 4, IRAQ

0700 HOURS, OR

Crade is back in the OR working on the sterilizers. Denti and I are talking in a hushed whisper; we don't want Crade to hear us.

"The GOBs don't want to do the paperwork because it will make them look bad that one of their soldiers tried to commit suicide. It's like it never happened. I think all he had to do was see the chaplain once."

At the mention of that I laugh. I know it's inappropriate, but sending a suicidal Satanist to a priest to make him feel better doesn't seem like the best thing to do.

"That's it?" I whisper back to Denti. "The man tries to kill himself and they don't even take his weapon away? They're just going to let things go on as usual?"

Crade walks in the room and Denti and I shut up. Crade looks at us and we give him a head nod. He grabs a notebook from the shelf and heads back to where he was. Denti and I look at each other; neither of us knows what to say to Crade.

Denti grabs a cinnamon bun off my plate.

"He's working fourteen hours every day, too; Gagney's making him. No more days off or time off."

"So instead of giving a suicidal man the attention he needs, he's given extra duty and told to move on."

"That's right . . ." Denti says back to me. "And I heard Gagney talking to someone saying that he thinks Crade probably just did it to make him look bad."

"That narcissistic. . . ."

Crade walks in and puts back the notebook he got a minute earlier. We both nod at him again.

2345 HOURS, MY ROOM

I look over at my nightstand and see: a bottle of sleeping pills, a full container of NyQuil, and a pack of cigarettes. My first pack of cigarettes. I went to the store today and they were fully stocked because they just got a big shipment in. I bought two bottles of NyQuil and Marlboro Reds. Lately I've been noticing that I crave cigarettes more often, and that I sleep a lot better after I have a cigarette, a sleeping pill, and a shot of NyQuil. Tonight, though, I don't feel like taking my sleeping pills or NyQuil. I feel like just being with my thoughts about what's going on. I stay up all night playing guitar and thinking about life and death. Eventually my mind grows tired and I begin to sleep.

0145 HOURS, MY ROOM

I can barely see their faces. I wake up from my dream and grab my photo album. In my dream I could no longer see the faces of my family and friends. I'm scared. I can't picture a single person from my past, from my life before the war. I can't see a single face. I look at my pictures and suddenly they come back to me. My mind fills with nostalgia from the times I'd spent with them. Everything and everyone seems so distant, no more real than a movie or a TV show. My head becomes filled with a cloud of haze as the drowsy night air tries to force me back to sleep. I slowly concede and lay my head down and drift off, but I now have the faces of my family and friends visible in my head again. I can only imagine how much worse it must be for Crade. To dream of the face of his child that he has never seen and may never see. I have pictures, but he has nothing. Who wouldn't go into a slight depression?

WEEK 3, DAY 1, IRAQ

2000 HOURS, AUDITORIUM

The MWR (morale, welfare, and recreation) group has decided to throw another talent show, this time with a PG rating. No dancing allowed; it's strictly a talent show with a few singers, a few people on guitar, and a few comedians thrown into the mix.

Captain Tarr is on stage singing a Peter, Paul and Mary song. She's quite a good singer, too. And even though she's not the best-looking woman in the unit, there is a group of young men hooting and hollering in the back.

"And next up will be Specialist Wilson," the person announcing the show proclaims.

Specialist Wilson, the mentally challenged soldier whose dick Colonel Lessly said he wanted to suck, is now on stage singing a Britney Spears song "Baby One More Time." He is wearing a suit that makes him look like a combination of a Jehovah's Witness and an accountant. His diet of snow cones and popcorn seems to have given him twenty pounds since the last time I saw him in Wisconsin. His singing is horrendous, but he's so bad that the crowd loves it. By the time Wilson is done, everyone is screaming for an encore. Wilson bows and I can see his face is bright red, but he is smiling. He thinks the applause and shouts are genuine so he looks pleased.

"And next up will be Colonel Lessly . . ." the announcer proclaims.

I'm not sure if it was planned that way or if Lessly set it up, but Wilson rushes off the stage and the smile leaves his face as Lessly is announced and walks on the stage.

Lessly begins singing "Can't Get Enough of Your Love Baby" by Barry White. Lessly is also a great singer, and his years of sucking down . . . cigars . . . have given him a thick, raspy voice that makes him sound just like Barry.

2100 HOURS, AUDITORIUM

The show is just ending and everyone is yelling and screaming for more. They want Specialist Wilson to come back out and sing another song.

"Wilson. Wilson. Wilson. Wilson. Wilson."

He walks over to the soldier running the karaoke machine and whispers something in his ear.

"Anyway You Want It," by Journey, starts playing in the background and the crowd goes wild. Men start screaming, women throw their hands in the air, someone lights a lighter and holds it high.

Wilson gets on stage and starts singing. He starts dancing, too; he doesn't care about the no-dancing rule.

Wilson is moving and shaking his hips while the seams of his clothing hold on for dear life. He takes off his sports coat and throws it to someone in the audience. The audience is cheering; everyone is singing along, and he's dancing all over the stage. Everyone loves it, and we all stand and sing along.

Somehow he got by the censors.

WEEK 3, DAY 4, IRAQ

1600 HOURS, SLEEPING AREA

Mardine yells, "He must have jammed something into the other side of the door, or broke his key off in it."

One of the medics pushes past all of us. He takes the butt of his rifle and swings it like a baseball bat into the window.

The glass falls to the ground and the medic clears it all from the sill so that he can climb through the window.

Ten seconds later the door is kicked open. Ten seconds after that, he is dragging Crade's body from his room. It's limp, like a rag doll, and his face is ocean blue; he's not breathing.

"Clear the way!" First Sergeant Mardine yells as the ER medics load Crade onto the stretcher. A group has now formed around the area and everyone parts like the Red Sea as the stretcher and the ER medic run for the hospital.

"Nothing to see here. Everyone go back to what you were doing. Everybody get out of the way," First Sergeant Mardine yells trying to disperse the crowd.

1800 HOURS, HOSPITAL

I'm angry. Angry at Crade for doing this to himself. Angry at myself for not seeing the signs. Angry at Denti and me for only giving him a head nod when we should have asked him how he was feeling. Most of all I am angry at the GOBs and Gagney. A man is suicidal and the GOBs don't want to do the paperwork and send him home because it will make them look bad? Instead of giving him the help he needs, Gagney gave him extra duty and said that Crade was only doing it to make him look bad. People are only worried about themselves. I'm disgusted with their apathy.

Denti and I step into the hospital. He looks sad, but not like he's going to cry. I would say at this moment it would be impossible for him to cry; we're both carrying so much anger. Hudge is leaning forward in a chair with her head in her arms on the table. She looks up as we walk in.

She's been crying, but the tiniest of smiles spreads across her face when she sees us.

"He's going to be all right. The doctors said that if we weren't a hospital unit and didn't find him when we did, he'd be dead."

Denti and I sit down with Hudge. None of us talk; there's no need to. For the past two hours we've all heard every part of the story. We've all learned more about Crade than we have in all the past months.

He was depressed. He had been depressed for the past few weeks, and if there were any doubts about the first time being a suicide attempt there were none now. He broke his key in the door so no one could get in and was expecting to lay there and die in peace. He hated it here in Iraq. He hated Gagney. He hated the GOBs and the way they were running things. He missed his family, he wanted to see his son, and he and Hernley had been having relationship trouble.

I guess I can't say I was surprised that Crade tried to kill himself again. He was given extra duty and had to work longer hours than any of us. Hell, if I wasn't depressed I sure as hell would be after being given extra hours and longer days.

After his first attempt I wasn't sure how to address him. I wasn't sure how things had changed, but it felt different. Certain jokes are off limits, as are certain movies in the break room; everyone starts walking on eggshells. I gave Crade space, thinking that he could sort things out on his own. The irony is that all this most likely added to his depression.

"Anthony, they're going to send him home. . . . " Hudge looks my way, speaking for the first time in twenty minutes.

" . . . so he can get the right care he needs . . . and deserves. We've all got to watch him, stay with him for a few hours on suicide watch during the shifts. . . ."

I nod yes and we continue sitting in silence.

WEEK 3, DAY 5, IRAQ

1600 HOURS, ICU

"What am I supposed to do with him for four hours?" I ask Denti.

"Play cards with him, read a book, watch a movie—I don't know," he says.

I grab a book from the bookshelf and head toward the ICU. Hernley and Crade are sitting there watching a movie on a laptop.

They're both sitting on the bed together and laughing, as if nothing ever happened. I try to act as if everything is cool, and I don't tell them why I'm there. But they know, so I sit down and read my book while they finish the movie. A few minutes later Hernley goes back to work.

"Hey, now don't go killing yourself on my watch," I chuckle.

An awkward silence follows and Crade stares at me expressionless. I decide to follow it up with something else.

"What . . . too soon for those jokes?"

Another awkward silence follows, but this one seems more deliberate. Crade cracks a smile, I smile back at him, and we both give a lighthearted laugh. I can see in his eyes that he wants to talk. I reach into my pocket and take out a deck of cards that Denti gave me.

"Rummy 500?" I say.

"Let's do it," Crade replies.

I'm supposed to be there making him not want to kill himself, as if suddenly playing a game of Rummy 500 with me will give him a new perspective on life. Hell, with all the tension, anxiety, and awkwardness in the room, after a few hours I might want to kill myself.

WEEK 4, DAY 4, IRAQ

1300 HOURS, OR

I remember when I was a little kid I had a goldfish named Spike. I had Spike for a week before he died, and before I even got a chance to properly mourn Spike's death my parents bought me a new fish. Crade has only been gone for a few days and his replacement is already here: Specialist Cather. Cather is a tall black man with hands the size of those foam fingers you see at sporting events. He is fifty-eight years old and is the same rank as me—which I know is impressive, because it's not easy to be that old and still be at such a low rank.

Today, on Cather's first day, we've decided to throw him on first shift so that he can get acquainted with the speed of the cases.

With Cather's old age and gigantic hands, he's a disaster. Many cases we work with require fine, delicate instruments, and Cather's bulbous hands are too large to grasp the tiny instruments. Cather is on his third case today and he tells me he's done trying.

"I'll tell ya, Anthony. I'm too old for this stuff. I think I'll just clean instruments from now on. Or maybe Gagney can put me in charge of the inventory or something for the move—now that I can do."

WEEK 4, DAY 7, IRAQ

1300 HOURS, OR

When we first heard we were moving Gagney had us do an inventory count. Then two weeks later he had us do another, then another, then another, each time swearing that it would be the last. And every time we do an inventory we all end up working between twelve to sixteen hours every day for a week. The unit that's taking over our hospital came in last night. They want us to do a full inventory of all the equipment we're signing over to them.

Reto and I stop unloading equipment from the conex to take a cigarette break. I take the pack out of my pocket.

We take long, slow drags. Denti finally gets back after over an hour.

"Hey, what is it, break time? You guys were supposed to be working while I was gone."

"What, are you kidding me? I'm supposed to be on second shift. I'm not even supposed to be here right now, but I'm working while you're inside doing God knows what," Reto is yelling.

"Relax," Denti replies. "You hear one of the members of their unit has already been caught having sex with someone from our unit?" Denti laughs to himself. "It was that hillbilly girl, too, Specialist Bane."

At the mention of Specialist Bane, Reto nods his head and I laugh. Bane is probably one of the most slovenly soldiers in our unit. She has grease permanently caked in her hair and spends her days retelling Jeff Foxworthy jokes. I take pleasure in hearing that Bane slept with a soldier from the new unit, partly because it makes our unit look bad to the other unit and it's like wearing a badge of honor, and also because Bane is Specialist Boredo's girlfriend.

✚

BBBAAAMMMM!!!
BBBBAAAAMMMM!!!!
BUNKERS! BUNKERS! BUNKERS!
Maybe, I suppose, we won't be leaving soon enough.

MONTH 5

"I WASN'T PREPARED FOR THIS."

WEEK 1, DAY 4, ANBAR PROVINCE, IRAQ

1300 HOURS, NEW BASE

We're finally at our new base. The luscious trees and chirping birds we lived with in the northern part of Iraq are gone. They've been replaced with two trees and lots of sand. This is the Iraq that people picture in their heads if they've never been here: open spaces, buildings no higher than two stories, and massive sandstorms.

This former Marine base is much bigger and the buildings are more spread apart than what we've been used to. The dining facility and the hospital are now further away from our rooms. Actually, our new hospital still hasn't been built yet. One of the supply lines bringing us the parts was hit and it delayed the whole process. We were told to sit tight and relax given that there's nothing to do—and to check in twice a day with Gagney. He has decided that we need to check in with him whenever we go anywhere and then every couple of hours even if we don't. In the morning before and after breakfast we check in, the same for lunch, dinner, and when we go to the gym or the community room.

WEEK 1, DAY 7, IRAQ

1300 HOURS, MY ROOM

Torres and Denti are now my roommates, along with Markham. There are four of us, or I suppose five of us. Torres's girlfriend,

Cardoza, has decided to spend most her nights with him, bunking in our room. They spend most of their time watching movies and giggling.

A National Guardsman named Tom, who lives next door to us and has been here sixteen months with two more left on his tour, is starting to make me afraid:

"We'd been in Iraq for a year and it was time to go home. We sent all of our stuff back—books, uniforms, movies, laptops, radios—everything. We loaded all of our gear onto the plane, had our orders in hand, and then it happened. An officer came aboard the plane, looked at us, and said, 'Unlock boys, we just got extended for another six months.' That was four months ago. A television station even did a story on us, after a bunch of our families complained back home. But nothing happened; you know how it is. It's the military. We have no choice."

Tom keeps talking, and I don't want to hear what he has to say. I don't want to even imagine getting extended another six months. I want a choice.

WEEK 2, DAY 2, IRAQ

1700 HOURS, AUDITORIUM

Mandatory meeting: While our hospital is being built, the GOBs have decided to do some unit restructuring. We're waiting for the changes to be announced. Reto is sitting next to me, and we started playing tic-tac-toe. He won one game, I've won once, and we've tied eleven times.

"Let's give a big round of applause for Command Sergeant Major Ridge," Colonel Jelly says from the stage. There are two hundred of us in the room and six people clap. Colonel Jelly announces that Command Sergeant Major Ridge is retiring and that we're getting a new command sergeant major in a few days.

"You know what's really going on, right?" Reto says as he places an *X* at the top right.

"No, what?" as I place an *O* in the middle.

"The unit that replaced us in Mosul made a complaint to the IG about us. They complained that we took all the equipment and left them with nothing."

It's true; we did take everything with us: from coffee makers and televisions to tongue depressors and bandages—anything that we could fit into our bags. When we first arrived in Mosul, it was completely stocked, but when we left, we weren't sure if the new base and hospital would be supplied, so we took everything with us. Reto and I start another game.

I place an *O* at the bottom left.

"They're forcing him out. You can't retire a sergeant major while in-country."

Colonel Jelly announces that First Sergeant Powell will be leaving us, too, and will be doing an administrative job in another unit—which is another way of firing someone and also using that person as a scapegoat without specifically saying so.

"So that's three," Reto says to me.

I'm not sure if he's talking about tic-tac-toe or what.

"That's three—two command sergeant majors and one first sergeant axed," Reto goes on.

"They got rid of CSM Fellows—"

"Powell and Ridge. That just doesn't happen—"

A soldier in front of us turns around. She's an older lady, a major, and she doesn't look pleased, either because Reto and I are talking or because someone we mentioned is a friend.

Colonel Jelly's glasses are falling toward the tip of his nose and he is staring at his note cards that lie on the podium. His eyes don't look up.

"And, with first sergeant Powell leaving, the southern hospital will no longer have its own First Sergeant, or command sergeant major. Instead, in a few days we will have one sergeant major for hospitals, north and south. Also, on a personal note I would like to congratulate Staff Sergeant North and Captain Dillon on their wedding. Unfortunately Captain Dillon will no longer be our company commander, but let's give her a round of applause; she's done a great job. And also let's give a round of applause for your new company commander, Captain Cardine." Three people clap, and two yell sarcastically. I remember her well from signing the CAB papers for her.

Colonel Jelly is referring to Captain Dillon, our company commander, and her husband, Staff Sergeant North. Captain Dillon got her position by lying. Before we left for Iraq, our unit had to do inventory. Our company commander was Captain Bodan. He did the inventory and found that we were almost a million dollars short. When he brought his concerns up to the GOBs, they told him to sign for it anyway. Bodan refused. Captain Dillon (at the time she was a lieutenant) overhears all of this and comes up with a plan. She told the GOBs that if they promote her to captain and then company commander, she will sign for the equipment saying it's all there, even when it's not. The GOBs agreed, and that's how she became our company commander.

Staff Sergeant North, who got caught reading someone else's mail, and Dillon have been married for over a year, but when they left for Iraq they said they weren't married. That way they were able to get separate BHAs (basic housing allowance: a military program that helps pay your mortgage or rent while you're fighting). North and Dillon, who are paying the mortgage on the house that they lived in, filed separate BHAs and thus got twice the money for their mortgage. Because this is illegal, someone rightly complained. It is also illegal for North and Dillon to be in the same chain of command and married. The military really frowns on this. Since Captain Dillon was the company commander she was North's boss. It's the commander's job to hand out orders, and during a time of war those orders could often mean the difference between life and death. If there's a dangerous mission, a commander isn't going to send his or her spouse on it; the commander is going to send someone else. Fortunately, though, the IG found all of this out and Dillon will be relieved of command.

"You know she's not getting in trouble either," Reto says to me, forgetting to whisper.

"Shhh. What do you mean?"

The soldier in front of us looks back again.

"Well, she's getting relieved of her position, yeah. But that's it." Her and North have cheated the government out of tens of thousands of dollars and they lied to the Army, but she's only being moved to an administrative job in the unit command.

"And look over there." Reto points his finger to the left of the room at Staff Sergeant North and Captain Dillon. "The GOBs even allowed Sergeant North to come up here from the southern hospital so that they can be together."

"Will you please be quiet, I am trying to listen," the woman in front of us says to Reto.

"That's four," I whisper, holding up four fingers.

"Four what?" Reto replies.

"Soldier, you heard me!" the woman repeats. Reto and I are silent. Even though we are being relieved of two command sergeant majors, one first sergeant, and one company commander, we know nothing will change. The GOBs are the problem. The meeting continues, and Colonel Jelly ends by telling us that our new command sergeant major is Sergeant Major Lavaled.

WEEK 2, DAY 4, IRAQ

1730 HOURS, AUDITORIUM

Command Sergeant Major Lavaled has a slight resemblance to Command Sergeant Major Ridge. He has a muscular jawbone and a slowly wrinkling face, but the similarities end there. His hair is a dark gray color that could pass for black, and he has a tiny sliver of a patch of white hair on the top left side of his head. He's from the southern part of the United States. His laugh is fake and not infectious—and when he gives a speech no one is moved. He tells us about the little things in our unit that he's going to change, but he's trying to make it sound like a big deal.

"Also, soldiers, I have a few things that I want to bring up with you," Lavaled says.

"From now on when you go to the dining facility, I want you all to eat with your weapons strapped on you at all times. NO putting them on the ground or putting them in the weapons rack. You must keep them on you at all times. And also, I know that some of you are excited about the fact that there is no more guard duty here because the Ugandan soldiers have taken it over, but I want all sergeants and below to still do guard duty. Just watch the Ugandan soldiers and make sure they do everything right. Besides, I've heard about your unit, and it might not be the worst thing if some of you don't have too much free time."

Reto and I turn to look at each other. One of the things we had been looking forward to about our new base was that there'd be no more guard duty.

The hospital will be open in a few days.

WEEK 2, DAY 5, IRAQ

2000 HOURS, AUDITORIUM

"This better be good!" Denti says to Reto and me as we enter the auditorium. There's a talent show scheduled for tonight, and I had to convince these two to come with me.

"First up, we will have John and Blake singing and playing the guitar," the emcee announces. Two Marines get on stage and they begin singing and playing the song "Cold" by Crossfade.

2030 HOURS, AUDITORIUM

"Next up we have Captain Tarr singing a song by Janis Joplin."

Reto, Denti, and I laugh as five Marines in the back of the room begin hollering and calling Captain Tarr by her first name—which the emcee hadn't mentioned.

Captain Tarr sings, and she's as good as last time. The emcee then gets back on the mic and announces the next performer.

"And next up we have Colonel Lessly, who will be singing 'Baby One More Time' by Britney Spears and 'Any Way You Want It' by Journey."

Colonel Lessly gets on stage and looks in the audience at Reto, Denti, and me. We are the only other members of our unit that are here.

"This song goes out to a friend of mine, Larry," Lessly says. Larry is Specialist Wilson's first name.

Reto and I look at each other and a chill goes up my spine. Those are the same songs Wilson sang at the last talent show. Lessly begins singing and dancing just the way Wilson danced on stage when everyone cheered him on.

"Let's get the hell out of here," Denti says.

It's too creepy to watch an old man sing a song dedicated to a mentally challenged kid whose dick he tried to suck, so the three of us grab our weapons and leave the auditorium.

WEEK 3, DAY 1, IRAQ

1300 HOURS, OUR NEW HOSPITAL

"Our hospital is now officially open and ready for business. . . . We have a fully functioning four-bed OR that is ready to go . . . along with. . . ."

Actually that's BS.

Colonel Jelly is standing on a makeshift stage in front of a crowd of three hundred people. Everyone from our unit is here as well as dozens of military commanders—from one-, two-, and three-star generals to colonels and sergeant majors from all the bases in Iraq.

I look over at Reto, then at Denti, Torres, Chandler, and Hudge; down the line everyone shakes their head no to me. Colonel Jelly is lying to everyone here, but we were told to keep our mouths shut. Jelly and the GOBs want to open the hospital early so they will look good—that's why we're having this ceremony. The fact of the matter, however, is that we only have two OR beds. We're still waiting on parts for the fourth, and the third one is only partially set up. Colonel Jelly knows this, but instead he has chosen to lie.

I know I should say something, but I can't. Who would I talk to? I only know that if we have more than two patients at a time we're screwed. It's been a while since I've done this, but I close my eyes and pray. I pray and I don't ask for an end to the war. I simply ask that we don't get more than two surgical patients at a time.

In his speech, Command Sergeant Major Lavaled says, "I'd like to thank all the soldiers out there who helped make this possible. I know we couldn't have gotten the chance to open this hospital if we hadn't done such a great job in Mosul. We deserve this, and I'm glad with our hard work we can open this hospital early."

Even though Command Sergeant Major Lavaled has only been in our unit for a few days, already he is acting as though he has been with us the whole time, as if he was in all those surgeries with us. He's another one I'll try to give the benefit of the doubt.

WEEK 3, DAY 2, IRAQ

0900 HOURS, OR

I can handle doing surgeries on Iraqis and Americans because we put ourselves in this mess . . . but a dog? After seeing it lying on the table, brought over from the K-9 unit, its big brown eyes wide open, I almost start crying. I forget to block my emotions. Then a nine-year-old Iraqi child is brought in. She's got shrapnel wounds to the stomach and leg. I wasn't prepared for this.

WEEK 3, DAY 7, IRAQ

1600 HOURS, OUTSIDE THE OR

As Laveled approaches, I get into the position of parade rest—hands behind my back, legs shoulder-width apart.

"Good evening, command sergeant major."

"Good evening, soldier. Hot day out today. Good thing I'm not wearing any underwear."

I know that I should laugh as a sign of respect, but I can't. Command Sergeant Major Lavaled says nothing. We both stare at each other, holding the other's eye contact. I'm in no mood to play this game.

Twenty seconds goes by: *What the hell is going on? Is he going to just stand here staring at me?*

Thirty seconds: *Why didn't I just laugh at his stupid joke?*

Forty-five seconds: *It's too late now. I can't laugh; I'll just look like an idiot.*

Fifty-five seconds: *I'm insane. I need to do something.*

"At least I don't get any wedgies this way," he says after almost a minute of eye contact.

I continue to stare at him. *Why is he just staring at me?*

Twenty seconds: *What is this guy's fucking problem? Leave me alone you freak show!*

Thirty seconds: *Maybe I don't understand the joke.*

Forty-five seconds: *I wonder what he's thinking. Is the whole under-wear wedgie thing some type of gay code?*

One minute: *If it is some type of code, then maybe I shouldn't be staring at him. He'll think I'm leading him on. I'm sure Gagney will love that. The CSM will think I'm a tease.*

"I mean sometimes I get swamp ass, so I just do lunges and dry it up," he says.

What the fuck is going on? This doesn't even make sense. I don't think he's gay.

Ten seconds: *I can't believe I'm having a staring contest with the new CSM.*

Twenty seconds: *Does this fucking guy really need my approval that bad that he'd have a staring contest with me until I act subservient and laugh?*

Thirty seconds: *Oh my god, my eyes are watering. I can't let him see me cry or avert eye contact. I heard somewhere that in prison that means you're someone's bitch.*

Thirty-five seconds: *I've got to do something.*

Forty seconds: *I've got it!*

I move the right side of my mouth up a half centimeter into what could be called a smirk.

Five seconds. . . .

Lavaled looks at me and smiles.

"All right, very well, soldier; carry on with the day's work."

Oh dear God, I need to get out of here.

WEEK 4, DAY 4, IRAQ

1400 HOURS, OR

I notice that if I smoke four Camel Light cigarettes one after the other and try to walk, I get all woozy and I feel like I'm drunk. Although it's been a while since I bought my first pack of cigarettes, I just bought my first carton. The feeling that I get when I down four Camel Lights is amazing. It relaxes me and puts me in my head—but there's really no point unless you're going to smoke a few right in a row.

"Hey, you want to go grab a smoke?" Reto asks me, already knowing the answer. I love smoking a cigarette and writing in my journal. I love smoking during smoke breaks. I love smoking after a good meal. I love smoking before I go to bed. I love smoking in the morning.

✚

Reto and I take a ladder outside at the back of the OR and go up on the roof.

"Hey, someone give me a hand up," Denti yells up to Reto and me. We help him up and finish our cigarettes. We call this our clubhouse.

1445 HOURS, OR

"Did you step in something?" Reto looks.

"I didn't step in anything."

We're emptying a small trash bucket from the bathroom into a larger one.

"Eww—"

"What is that, toilet paper?"

Inside the trash barrel there are dozens of rolled up pieces of toilet paper with shit on them.

"Who's been throwing their toilet paper into the trash? Why don't they just flush it?"

MONTH 6

"WE ARE IN THE MIDDLE OF FIGHTING A WAR AND OUR LEADER HAS GIVEN HIMSELF A MONTH-LONG VACATION."

WEEK 1, DAY 4, IRAQ

1445 HOURS, OR

A conversation between Dr. Bill and Colonel Reke:

"Are you sure they're the right patients?" Colonel Reke's face is stone, but her wavering voice gives her away: She's concerned about something.

"No, they're all dead. Every single one of them. Routine wounds and we saved their lives."

Dr. Bill has just finished a follow-up call on nine of his Iraqi patients that he's done surgery on.

WEEK 1, DAY 6, IRAQ

1450 HOURS, OR

"You have got to be kidding me. Not again." Reto holds up a trash bag and inside there are rolled up pieces of toilet paper with shit on them.

"What the hell is going on here?"

"I don't know, man, but whenever we empty out the trash—I'm sick of smelling this."

Reto and I grab the trash and double bag it, vowing to catch whoever is doing this. We know it's neither of us, because, A, we're the ones who have to clean it up, and, B, we both agreed that if we had to take a shit we'd go in another section's bathroom so we wouldn't smell up ours.

Reto and I throw the trash in the trash bin and walk back into the hospital.

I go into the bathroom and put on a teeth-whitening strip. I bought a box of thirty-day teeth whiteners, and I use them at the end of every shift to counter the effects of cigarettes and coffee. Some of the top strips have gone missing. Who would steal teeth-whitening strips? I make it my mission to notice who has notice-ably whiter teeth.

WEEK 2, DAY 2, IRAQ

1445 HOURS, OR

Today: three surgeries, four amputations, and two GSWs. Reto and I are vegging in the break room.

Lieutenant Hamilton sticks her head in the door.

"Hey, have you guys seen Colonel Jelly?"

Reto's eyes are closed and his head is nodding up and down. He's trying not to fall asleep.

"There was a huge herpes sore across Lieutenant Hamilton's lips," I say.

"You're crazy, man. I didn't see anything," Reto says. His eye-lids fall back down and he starts lightly snoring.

WEEK 3, DAY 1, IRAQ

2230 HOURS, SLEEPING AREA

I put down the book that I'm reading. It's *A Long Walk to Freedom*, by Nelson Mandela. I need to take a break; it's the longest book I've ever read, and it's too much to take in all at once. I look over at my roommates. Markham is sitting on his bed. He's got huge earmuff headphones on and he's playing the guitar. I stand up and look over at Denti. He's lying in bed with tiny headphones on watching *Family Guy*. Denti is laughing, and as he laughs I check out his teeth to see if they possibly look whiter than normal. I turn toward Torres. He and Cardoza are snuggled up together on his bed. Neither Torres nor Cardoza have headphones on, and I can hear that they're watching a movie. I look once more at the three of my roommates. I need something to do.

Markham is jamming on the guitar now and I don't want to disturb him. I look at Denti; he's laughing at an episode of *Family Guy* and I don't want him to disturb me. I walk over toward Torres and Cardoza; Cardoza is talking and Torres is listening intently. I think for being at war, we all haven't lost our senses of humor.

"What are you guys watching?"

"Hey, Michael," Cardoza is smiling. She's always smiling. "We're watching *Wedding Crashers*. But hey . . . I was just telling Torres something about Colonel Jelly. You'll appreciate this story. . . ."

It's been happening more and more: I'm getting tired of hearing stories about everyone. I just don't care. I'm sick of hearing about husbands cheating on their wives and wives cheating on their husbands.

"You know Lieutenant Hamilton, right?" Cardoza begins.

"All right, all right, tell me."

"Well, yesterday. . . ."

Someone begins knocking on the door.

"It's pretty late for someone to be knocking."

I get up and open the door.

"AANNTTHHOONNYY." Standing in front of me is Specialist Fangell. I give him a hug and bring him into my room. Torres and Cardoza see him and jump up to give him hugs as well.

Fangell is an OR medic from our southern hospital, and he's been allowed to come up here for a few days and train with us. Fangell is six feet tall, twenty years old, and is a former Banana Republic model. He is wearing a cutoff tank top that shows off a tattoo on his right shoulder. It's an Army Special Forces tattoo. He got the tattoo when he was eighteen and full of dreams to join the Special Forces, just like his uncle. But Fangell isn't in the Special Forces. He's an operating room medic in an Army Reserve unit, and now he has a tattoo on his shoulder of a unit he was never in.

Fangell starts talking, but after a few minutes I start to daydream.

"Anyways, I was wondering if you guys could help me out. I wanted to say hi to Colonel Jelly—"

"I thought he was down south, visiting you guys," I say, coming out of my daydream.

"Haha," Cardoza laughs. "You guys don't know where he's been?"

"Well, we're not his personal secretaries," I say sarcastically, looking at Cardoza. She is one of Jelly's secretaries so she is privy to information that only Jelly and the GOBs know.

"He sure as hell isn't at our southern hospital. I was told he was up here," Fangell jumps in.

"That's because he's not," Cardoza replies. "He just wants everyone up north to think that he's visiting the southern hospital. And he wants everyone down south to think that he's up north. In actuality he's back in the States going to war college. He has to go if he wants to be promoted to general or something."

"Baby, are you kidding me?" Torres says as he grabs Cardoza by the waist and spins her around.

"He doesn't want anyone to know, though. The school lasts for about a month and he's already been there for two weeks."

"We are in the middle of a fucking WAR. In the middle of this Goddamn dessert and our 'leader' is back home in the States."

"No wonder why he lied to everyone. He doesn't want everyone to know that he gave himself a month-long vacation," Fangell says.

I start to feel nauseous—we are in the middle of fighting a war and our leader has given himself a month-long VACATION. We don't even have a leader in this GODFORSAKEN COUNTRY!

2300 HOURS, SLEEPING AREA

By the time I come back inside the room I've had three cigarettes, and Cardoza, Torres, and Fangell have changed the topic of conversation.

I lay down on my bed.

"So, I am outside of my room a few days ago," I hear Cardoza finishing the story she started telling me, "and I'm waiting for Hudge so we can go to the gym together. Well, she was late and as I'm outside waiting I see Lieutenant Hamilton and a guy knocking on someone's door. The door opens and one of the doctors from the ER comes out. Hamilton and the guy go inside. Two minutes later Hamilton and the guy walk by me. They both have these herpes sores all over their mouths and lips."

I turn over in my bed and throw the pillow over my ears as Cardoza—continues talking about all the people in our unit who've gotten STDs.

WEEK 4, DAY 1, IRAQ

1430 HOURS, OR

We now have the pieces to all four of our OR beds, so now we officially have the four beds operational. It's been a month since Jelly gave that speech. Although we had a mini mass casualty, it wasn't anything we couldn't handle and it was mostly taken care of in the ER. I don't know what I would have done, though, if commanders sent us patients thinking we had four beds when we only had two. People probably would have died and it would have been my fault for not speaking up. I'm glad I don't have to worry about it anymore.

Reto and I grab the trash from the bathroom and again there is toilet paper with huge chunks of shit loaded in there. It sucks, but we've come up with a plan to catch the person, or at least stop him, and tonight we are going to implement it.

Reto picks up the bathroom trashcan and places it outside the bathroom, three feet away against the wall. He looks at me and I smile in approval. Our trap is set. Whoever is throwing their shitty toilet paper into the garbage will have to open the bathroom door, walk out, and place it into the trash. Reto takes the bags and heads outside to put them in the dumpster. I head back into the bathroom and put on a teeth-whitening strip.

I've been using my teeth-whitening strips for about three weeks now and I have one week left of lower strips, but I only have one single upper strip left. I'm still not sure who is taking them, but now I spend all day looking at my coworkers' teeth to see if the top ones look any brighter from day to day. I have no idea who, but right now my attention is on Sergeant Sellers. She also bought teeth whiteners, and she keeps her box in a wide-open area whereas I keep my box hidden in the bathroom. I suspect that the culprit may initially be stealing from her and that she in turn steals the ones that she's missing from me.

Fangell is there waiting for me. I don't know how long he's been there, but he gives me a hug.

"Well, this is it, man. I've got to go back down to the southern hospital. It's been good. Take care."

"You too, man. It was great to see you," I reply.

Fangell turns and I watch him walk away. It's always sad to see a friend leave, and as he walks away I think back on all the stories he's told me since he's been up here. Men and women cheating on their husbands, wives, boyfriends, and girlfriends. I think of all the people he's told me about that are getting alcohol, and even cocaine and heroin, shipped to them. As Fangell turns a corner and leaves my view, I think of the worst stories that he told me. A male doctor was running the sick call for the southern hospital. Sick call is where people go who aren't seriously injured but just sick, like the flu or stomach problems. They can come in and get care and medicine. A female soldier came in with complaints of flu-like symptoms, runny nose, fever, and headache. The doctor told her to lie down on the bed and he begins giving her a medical exam, but the doctor wasn't wearing any gloves. The exam consisted of him caressing her breasts and asking her to get naked, bend over, and cough. The female patient did what the doctor asked. When she left she immediately filed a complaint. Soon another woman came forward saying a few days earlier the same doctor did the same thing when she only came in for a headache.

Fangell is gone and I remember that I never got to hear how the story ends.

MONTH 7

"THE ARMY CAN'T ORDER ME TO PUT SOMETHING IN MY BODY."

WEEK 1, DAY 6, IRAQ

1430 HOURS, OR

I dump the contents from the package I received on the table: tuna fish, ramen noodles, a pair of used black socks, a notebook with half of the pages missing, and a pack of crayons from the family restaurant, Friendly's. The package says it's from a senior citizens group home in New Jersey.

I remember watching a news special on NBC a few years ago. It was about elderly people who were poor and didn't have enough money to pay for all their bills; from medicine to food to heating. Some of them could only take a pill once a day that was prescribed for three times a day. Some could only afford to eat tuna fish for every meal of the day, while others were forced to eat dog food.

I put away the food in the OR break-room cupboards; they're filled with supplies sent to us from dozens of soldier support groups across the United States. I eat better here in Iraq than I do at home.

These people are sending us everything they have, and most of us don't deserve it. They aren't sending provisions to the heroes they think we are. It is going to us doing shit jobs and others who are criminals; people doing drugs, committing crimes, molesters, adulterers; people doing anything they can to only help themselves. The worst part about these old people sending me this package is they think they're helping. I don't want to tell anyone the truth because it will just break their hearts.

WEEK 2, DAY 1, IRAQ

0600 HOURS, MY ROOM

Beep. Beep. Beep.

I know that cigarettes are bad for you. They're bad for your health; they're bad for your skin, your teeth, and all of your internal organs. They're addictive, and I know I've slowly become addicted.

When my head is throbbing, I can hear the vessels in my brain pumping blood. It's as if tiny people are in my head trying to hammer their way out. I light up a Camel Light, and my headache goes away.

Cigarettes work; don't kid yourself. They bring me to another place. They relax me. People say that in life we're either running away from pain or toward pleasure. Well, cigarettes combine both: They hide you from the pain and stress and they move you toward instantly gratifying pleasure. I'm not sure how much I smoke, and I don't really care. Not anymore. I'll quit when I get home. I'm only going to smoke in Iraq. I make a mental note to quit the second I get back to Boston.

WEEK 2, DAY 7, IRAQ

0600 HOURS, MY ROOM

Steak. That means it's Wednesday. Every Wednesday is steak day. You know what? I don't even need a watch. I broke mine a little over a month ago, and I'm too cheap to buy a new one. But it doesn't even matter. My biological clock is set, fixed, and repaired. I wake up at the appropriate time and head to work, and I then stay there until the next shift comes in and then I go home. On schedule. First time, every time. I write in my journal every night and it doesn't matter if I don't know the exact date. I've been rebooted. I know when it's going to be steak day. And that's Wednesday.

WEEK 3, DAY 5, IRAQ

1700 HOURS, OR

"The ultimate measure of a man is not where he stands in moments of comfort and convenience, but where he stands at times of challenge and controversy."

—Martin Luther King Jr.

I think Martin Luther King Jr. is right. A man's true character can only be tested when he's pushed to his limits. That's where the true test of manhood comes from. It has nothing to do with age or social status, only how you act when put to the test. How you deal with the test is then who you truly are.

Gagney walks in the room:

"There is a mandatory meeting tomorrow at 1400 hours. You will all be there!"

Reto continues searching Google for the price of a pool table. "We're working tomorrow."

"Did I ask you if you were working? No! I know you are working."

"We can't just leave the OR—"

"You will all be there because this is a mandatory meeting!

"Take a pager with you guys. If there's an emergency you'll be paged. Be there on time. In fact, be there early. I want you two the first ones there."

I can feel his anger linger in the room for minutes after he's gone.

WEEK 3, DAY 6, IRAQ

1445 HOURS, AUDITORIUM

"Listen to me, soldiers; it is mandatory for everyone to get an anthrax shot." Colonel Jelly stands on stage in front of our entire unit.

"It is a series of six shots known as the Anthrax Vaccine Immunization Program, otherwise known as the AVIP. You must all get the shots within the next three days. That is a direct order! OR ELSE!" Colonel Jelly is actually not looking at anyone while he says this; instead he's reading from a script and staring at his shoes.

Since Reto and I essentially have the same thoughts because we've been through so much together, I know he's thinking, "Why add the inflection at 'OR ELSE?' Whenever we are given a direct order, we are just given an order and that's it. It's assumed that the order will be followed. Never has there been an 'OR ELSE' attached to the end."

A paper is thrust into our hands. It only has three things written on it:

1. The anthrax shot is mandatory.
2. The shot is FDA approved.
3. It is a series of six shots.

The meeting ends and we go back to work. If this was like the flu shot, there wouldn't be a whole production. We wouldn't have needed a meeting. We wouldn't have been given papers, and Colonel Jelly wouldn't be giving us a direct order.

1515 HOURS, OR

Reto is on the computer searching Google for "anthrax shot."

"Look, man, I haven't even opened the first link yet but all the top results look bad."

I look down at the computer screen. There are a handful of links to click on, and each one has a blurb about the site or an article related to anthrax.

American soldiers disciplined for not getting the anthrax shot: Is it safe? . . . American soldier dies after taking anthrax shot: More to come. . . . Anthrax shots now mandatory by the Pentagon: Adverse reactions cited . . . Gulf War Syndrome. . . . We click on one site after another. Reto is in one room on a computer. Hudge is in another doing the same thing. I'm at a third.

"Hey, come check this out," Reto yells to us. "Apparently the anthrax shot is FDA approved, but the company changed all the ingredients but still calls it by the same name."

"The FDA approved a series of three shots, not six." Hudge is saying.

Here's what else was found:

1. We are statistically thousands of times more likely to get sick from the anthrax shots taen we are to ever come in contact with any type of anthrax. And on top of that, the shot doesn't protect us against airborne anthrax.

2. There is a group of medical and military veterans that have evidence linking the anthrax shot to Gulf War syndrome from the first Gulf War.

3. As of 2006, 1.2 million troops have been given the anthrax shot, and of those 1.2 million, over 20,000 have been hospitalized because of direct complications due to the anthrax shot or some mysterious sudden illness that occurred after they'd gotten the shot.

4. The side effects can range from losing bone marrow and blood platelets to shrinking of the brain and Lou Gehrig's disease.

5. There has been ZERO research into the long-term effects of the anthrax shot.

1620 HOURS, OR

"I'm not taking it," Hudge says.

The Centers for Disease Control and Prevention had this to say about the shot and the reported frequency of side effects:

- Soreness, redness, or itching where the shot was given (about 1 out of 10 men, and about 1 out of 6 women)
- Muscle aches or joint aches (about 1 person out of 5)
- Headaches (about 1 person out of 5)
- Fatigue (about 1 out of 15 men and 1 out of 6 women)
- Chills or fever (about 1 person out of 20)
- Nausea (about 1 person out of 20)

Those aren't including the cases of the over 20,000 that were hospitalized.

We continue our research. . . .

1. Some soldiers who refused to take the shot report being held down against their will and given the shots.

2. The only reason the Army may be giving these shots is because they bought them during the first Gulf War and they're about to expire. They don't want them going to waste.

2245 HOURS, OR

"Who died in here?" Sergeant Sellers asks as she walks in the room.

It's time for the change of shift.

"Have a seat," Hudge says. She tells Sellers everything we've learned in the last eight hours. "We've all agreed to refuse the shot. Here, I'll leave this computer on and you and Waters can look over the information and decide what you want to do."

Reto, Denti, and I get up to leave; we've all made our decision not to take the shot and we will all take the consequences together—whatever Colonel Jelly meant by "OR ELSE."

2315 HOURS, MY ROOM

"Have you heard about these anthrax shots they're trying to make us take?"

I normally don't like to interrupt Markham while he's playing, but he's always been there for me and I need to talk to someone.

"We were at the OR on the computers doing research—"

Markham doesn't let me finish.

"Slow down."

"We're not going to take them."

"Do you know the consequences if you refuse to take it?"

"I don't know what they are. . . ."

"I have a friend that used to be in the Army. He was in the first Gulf War and he took the anthrax shots. He only got a series of three. He now has flulike symptoms for the rest of his life."

"Are you going to get it?"

"Hell no."

"How are you. . . ?"

"I'm exempt for being allergic to latex or something. But if I had to get the shot, I would refuse it. I think you're right."

"The Army can't order me to put something in my body."

"Dude, the U.S. Army can do whatever they want to you. You signed a contract; you gave up your rights."

WEEK 3, DAY 7, IRAQ

1445 HOURS, OR

When Reto and I get to work, Hudge and Denti are already waiting for us. They tell us they refused their shots. Reto and I walk over to the building where they're being administered, and we take a piece of paper off of a desk and sign our names. I'm not scared like I thought I'd be. I feel strong and safe in the decision.

2245 HOURS, OR

Shift ends and Sergeants Elster and Sellers come in for third shift. They tell us that they too have refused the shots. In fact, aside from Gagney, everyone in the OR has done so. Dozens and dozens of people from our unit have united on the issue: doctors, pharmacists, nurses, specialists, sergeants, colonels, majors, and master sergeants—they've all refused the shots. People have called home and talked to friends who are doctors or who have worked in the drug companies. *Without exception*, they were all told to not get the shot.

Colonel Loome, the highest-ranking person in the unit—and the person who suggested a mutiny while in Wisconsin—can be counted among us.

I've stood up to the Army: "NO. No, you may not put whatever you want in my veins. . . ."

WEEK 4, DAY 1, IRAQ

1500 HOURS, OR

When the statistics came in, it said a third of our unit refused to get the shot. When the GOBs heard about it they had a meeting, and then another with all the section leaders. When Gagney heard about half the unit refusing the shot, and the fact that 100 percent of his soldiers in the OR refused it, he didn't say anything at first; he just told us all to be at the OR at 1700.

1700 HOURS, OR

Gagney's reaction to the boycott of the anthrax shots:

"This is UN-FUCKING-BELIEVABLE!! My section is the only section that has 100 percent of the people refuse the shot! Listen to me! Getting this shot is a direct order from Colonel Jelly. Now I am also giving you a direct order: You get the shot. Are you trying to make me look bad!?! Is that it!?! Is that why you're refusing the shot!?! It's a shot! Let me tell you something. They'll prosecute you! I was at their meeting. You are refusing a direct order during a time of WAR! You can be fined and put in JAIL!!! YOU WILL BE FINED AND PUT IN JAIL. I will then make it my personal mission to make your lives a living hell! I can't even look at any of you."

"Oh yeah! Mandatory classes for anyone who refused the anthrax shot. Two different times for the next three days, you will make it to all of them." He slams the door.

✛

No one says anything. During our research we only studied the effects of getting the shot. Now we've heard the effects of not getting the shot. Refusing a direct order during a time of war does mean a fine; it also really does mean jail.

WEEK 4, DAY 2, IRAQ

1700 HOURS, ANTHRAX CLASS

One of the GOBs teaches the class. His method is to read from the pamphlet. I want to call him a thousand names. I want to tell him to look at our research. I want to call him a liar. But I sit quietly in my chair. The two doctors sitting next to me are also unimpressed. They don't seem to like him. No one likes the GOBs except the GOBs.

The consequences of not getting the anthrax shot:

"Colonel Jelly has ordered you to get this shot. That is a direct order from your unit commander. If you refuse to take the shot, best-case scenario, you will be kicked out of the Army with a dishonorable discharge—which follows you around like a felony— and fined thousands of dollars. Worst-case scenario . . . you will go to jail."

I look around and I see colonels, majors, captains, sergeants, staff sergeants, doctors, and nurses. People look scared, the GOB looks happy.

"Some of you have been in the military for twenty years; some have been in for two years. Let me tell you this. If you refuse this shot you will lose all your benefits that you've worked so hard for.

To the doctors out there, the Army paid for your schooling. You will have to pay that back. Those that have been in for twenty years and were planning on retiring, you can kiss your retirement goodbye. For those of you that were planning on going to school, no free tuition or GI Bill. Stop and think. Is refusing the shot really worth it? You deserve all the benefits you've received. You've worked hard to get to where you are now. Don't throw everything down the drain."

1800 HOURS, OR

"I don't want to lose my college benefits. I don't want to go to jail or lose pay," I say.

Reto stands. I can see in his eyes that he's already had these thoughts.

"Listen, man, I'll cover you. Go home and get some rest. Think things through. I'm refusing the shot no matter what. But I've got to tell you, I just talked to Hudge, and everyone else from the OR got the shot today. Denti, Elster, Waters. It's only you and me left," he says.

When I leave, I don't want Reto to see the weakness in my eyes. I smoke half a pack of cigarettes on the way to the room; once there, I down three sleeping pills and lay in bed.

For all I've said, for all I've not been able to do and hated it, I want someone to make this decision for me.

WEEK 4, DAY 3, IRAQ

0645 HOURS, SLEEPING AREA

Even people who have already received the shot, as well as those who have refused the anthrax shot, are required to attend Colonel Jelly's second meeting. People from down south will be there, including Staff Sergeant North. They received the shots a month ago and will be talking about it. Jelly is getting in trouble for so many of his soldiers refusing; I guess it looks bad when so many people from a medical unit are refusing to get a shot.

I laugh. Waking up this morning—from being so torn last night—and then hearing about the new meeting, my mind can't seem to handle everything that's going on and I just laugh. I laugh at the fact that we are fighting a war for freedom, and yet if we don't allow people to inject a potentially lethal liquid into our veins, we are being threatened with jail time. It's nothing if not ironic, and Reto is cracking up now, too.

0715 HOURS, AUDITORIUM

We are the last people to show up for the meeting, so we quietly make our way to the back of the room and sit down. Colonel Jelly has already read through the pamphlet and is again explaining the consequences of not taking the shot. He is also addressing the soldiers who have already gotten the shots and telling them not to let their friends throw their careers down the drain.

"Hey buddy, don't throw your career down the toilet." It's Reto. "Get the shot." I look at him and laugh. A soldier in front of me turns around; she smiles at Reto and then frowns at me. Colonel Jelly continues talking.

"Soldiers! I don't need to tell you again that this is a direct order. So let me just read you a list of the consequences for refusing the shots and a direct order during a time of war." Colonel Jelly says more of the same old. He adds that we will be dishonorably discharged from the military and that it will follow us around like a criminal record. His own recommendation is to push for the worst possible punishment:

"Refuse the shot the final time and you will most likely end up in jail. If you and a friend are both refusing the shot, make sure you're good friends because you could be sharing a jail cell. But really people, I want you to understand, the shots are safe. And to prove it we have Staff Sergeant North up here from our southern hospital who will tell us about their experiences with the shots."

Staff Sergeant North stands up. He has gained thirty pounds since the last time I saw him—only a few weeks ago at Colonel Jelly's meeting for unit restructuring.

"In our southern hospital we all had to take the anthrax shot and we conducted our own independent research." He's sweating like a hog. I can smell him from where I sit. He smells of bullshit.

"We had a pregnant soldier down south and we gave her the anthrax shot and then monitored her health. It's a month later and she's doing fine." He sits down and grins, obviously proud of himself. He has settled the score once and for all.

Is anyone else picking up that his pseudo-research is a little off? When the Army finds out that a woman is pregnant, they have to send her home as quickly as possible. Also, the pregnant soldier only received one out of a series of six shots.

The meeting ends with Colonel Jelly telling us that tomorrow and the next day will be the last two days to either get the shots or refuse them. After that, the consequences will be felt. Reto and I walk back to work.

0745 HOURS, OR

Reto and I head to the printer. We find the websites that we found earlier and make our own pamphlet on the real facts. We print off twenty copies. Hudge walks into the room and we hide the pamphlets.

"Hey guys, I want to talk. Listen, I got the shot and nothing happened to me. You guys are young. I just don't want to see you two throw your lives away."

Denti walks in:

"Listen, I'll say this quick. Don't be a fucking idiot. If they're going to send you to jail, just get the shot." Denti and Hudge leave. Reto goes to the bathroom.

Torres walks in.

"Michael. Listen, I'm sure you've heard this before. But I know these people are assholes for making us take these shots, but don't let them ruin you. Play their game for now, but that's it. I don't want to see anything happen to you. Reto has already made his decision; there's not much I can do . . . just think about it, okay? Weigh your options."

Reto knows that he might be refusing the shot alone. We print more pamphlets. Sergeants Elster and Sellers come in and relieve us. They also try to convince us to get the shots.

Reto and I leave. We don't talk. We take our pamphlets and methodically go into every male bathroom in our living quarters and hang the pamphlets on the walls. If refusing the shots weren't bad enough, we are now printing anonymous reading materials encouraging people to refuse a direct order. We know or can imagine the consequences, but we don't think of them. That is the only way you can do something. Focus on only doing what's right, not the consequences of any action. We are now fighting a new war.

✚

We go to our rooms. I turn my computer on and send an e-mail to my brother. I tell him to contact the press about what's going on. I then send an e-mail to my local and state representatives.

WEEK 4, DAY 4, IRAQ

0900 HOURS, OR

The next day people try to convince us to get the shots. Many of them call us idiots and say that we can't go against the Army. Some call us pansies and tell us to man up. Others come in and tell us that we're doing the right thing and that they wish they had the balls we have . . . and then they tell us to get the shot and not waste our careers.

The day goes on and more and more people get the shot, the main reason being that most don't want to lose their rank and throw away the careers they spent the last twenty years on. Dr. Bill comes in and says there are two patients on the way from the ER, GSWs. He then tells Reto and me that only a handful of people throughout our four-hundred-person unit have still refused the shot.

"Lot of good our fucking pamphlets did . . ." Reto says, turning around to grab instruments for the cases.

I tell him to be quiet and help him with the instruments. There have been a few people around the hospital talking about the pamphlets. They're the same people also saying that the GOBs are looking for those who did it. Reto and I have done research and found out that what we did (encouraging people to refuse a direct order) is considered mutinous and a jailable offense in itself, so even if we got the shots, we could still go to jail if anyone finds out that we hung the fliers.

1400 HOURS, OR

After a five-hour surgery, I am exhausted. I see Gagney and Reto sitting at a table in the break room. "Have a seat!" Gagney says.

I am in no mood to listen to his shit, but I slowly take a seat.

"Listen guys. Tomorrow is your final day to refuse. You and a few other idiots are the only ones left. Smarten up. Don't make things hard on yourselves. Do you want to go to jail? Be a good little soldier. Do what you're told" As he leaves, he is very calm.

"Oh, and by the way . . ." he says looking over his shoulder, "I looked it up in the regulations, and you can legally be shot for refusing a direct order during a time of war. We could take you out back and shoot you tomorrow; just something to think about, I know I have. . . ."

I look at Reto and I know that he won't back down. They can't use scare tactics to force us to take the shot. The question is no longer whether or not the shot is safe, it's do we succumb to their threats? We are here to be men and fight for our country, not for the land that it is on, but for the virtues that it stands on: liberty and freedom.

1500 HOURS, MY ROOM

It's comforting to finally know the answer. No more seesawing back and forth in my mind. On the way to our rooms Reto and I talk about sports, the weather, anything that will let our minds escape what's going on. When we get back to the room, I smoke four cigarettes and take three sleeping pills. Not surprisingly, I still can't sleep. I decide to go outside and smoke the rest of the cigarettes in my pack. I take two more pills. My mind is restless no matter what I do. I'm afraid I'll overdose. I look over at Markham in bed and I want to wake him up. I want to talk to him; I want him to tell me I'm doing the right thing. I lie back down.

My mind begins racing and echoing every thought and fear I've had over the past few days.

I figure the worst that can really happen is that I find myself in jail in a few days. I know I can handle jail. I will just spend my time reading and writing. Mandela was in jail for three decades.

The worst thing that could happen in jail is another inmate tries to rape me. I decide I won't let that happen and I'll die fighting. I might soon be dead because, worst-case scenario, I find myself in jail and someone tries to rape me . . . and I don't let them and I die fighting . . . and I don't die from a mortar attack or a terrorist . . . instead, I die for what . . . an ideal . . . a belief . . . is it worth it. . . ? is anything worth it. . . ?

WEEK 4, DAY 5, IRAQ

0900 HOURS, OR

It's 0900 and the sun is already shining. It hurts my eyes and burns my skin. Reto walks toward me, and I can tell by the bags under his eyes that he didn't sleep well either.

"I'm out of cigarettes," I say. He takes two out of his pack and hands me one. We light up.

"Listen, man, I'll understand if . . ." he trails off.

"Let's just go," my voice gives me away. I force myself to look at Reto, and I'm surprised to see that it looks like he wants to give in. He's silently begging me to give in.

We're not going to cave. We are going to refuse the shot for the final time. We know the possible consequences and we are ready.

Something starts happening after I realize that we'll actually be refusing for the final time. My body feels strange. I've never felt this before. I'm scared of the feeling, but I like it. My head is floating up as if it's attached to a balloon. My shoulders are back. Twenty-one years old and my father would be proud.

"You know, there's got to be some type of middle ground here. Things are never 100 percent black and white," Reto says.

"What do you mean?"

"Look, there's got to be some way we can beat them at their own game without getting the shots and without going to jail. . . ."

As soon as he says this, I think of something. I am a complete idiot. Reto is an idiot. I start laughing. Reto looks at me. I laugh harder. Reto is smiling.

"What, what, man? What's so funny . . . ?" I laugh harder. Reto is smiling a huge smile. He can tell I thought of something. I calm myself down enough to talk.

"We are fucking idiots."

"What, man?"

"This will work. Why the hell didn't you mention this middle ground shit before? You know you could have saved us a lot of worrying. And I could have saved about four packs of cigarettes. . . ."

"Tell me."

I grab two pieces of paper.

"Follow me."

We start walking.

"My roommate Markham doesn't have to get the shot because he had an adverse reaction to some shot and he's allergic to latex."

We walk in the hospital and toward the doctors' break room. I always knew that working side by side with these doctors day-in day-out would have its benefits.

I walk up to Dr. Bill with Reto following closely behind. We look like two schoolgirls, excited and giggling. I whisper in Bill's ear, hand him the two pieces of paper, and he hands them to a friend sitting next to him. The friend signs them. Reto and I are now allergic to latex. I almost cry as Reto and I run back toward the building for our anthrax shots. We hand our paper to the person who's supposed to be administering the shots, and we turn and run back to the OR.

Gagney stops us as we are entering the OR.

"Hey. Not so fast. Why are you two clowns smiling? Did you get those shots!?!"

Reto and I look at Gagney. Not even he can ruin this moment.

"Yeah, we took care of it," I say.

MONTH 8

"I NEED SOMETHING TO TAKE THE EDGE OFF."

WEEK 1, DAY 5, IRAQ

1800 HOURS, SLEEPING AREA

Socrates once said that the unexamined life is not worth living; however, he ended up having to kill himself because he wouldn't compromise his way of life. I wonder if it could then be said that he examined life and found it not worth living.

Today I'm celebrating my twenty-first birthday. Actually, my birthday was last month, but I didn't celebrate or mark the occasion. I think it's finally time for me to examine my life.

WEEK 1, DAY 7, IRAQ

2200 HOURS, OR

We've been on second shift for two days now and not a single case has come in; first shift, however, has been getting at least six a day. It's boring, which is why we are playing baseball inside the hall of the OR.

✚

"HOME RUN!!!" Reto yells as he throws his broom handle baseball bat to the ground and runs for first base on our makeshift field. I chase after the baseball, a rolled-up Ace bandage, and Reto runs from first to second base. "That's not a home run," I yell as

Reto goes from second to third base. "A home run is when you hit it over the door frame, and that was under it."

Reto doesn't listen and heads for home plate anyway, which is a crumpled up pair of pants.

The OR door slams. Reto and I look to see who it is to make sure that we're not getting in trouble. We invented our OR version of baseball yesterday, and we've already gotten three complaints about the noise. We look over, though, and are relieved when we see it's just Proust, a specialist and a medic in the ER. He's twenty-two but looks about seventeen—six feet tall, white, and has a pot belly and random tattoos all over his body. He also lived in my barracks in Wisconsin and always walked around naked. He also masturbated at least twice a day—I know this because he would announce it so that he could have some privacy in the bathroom. I didn't like the fact that he walked around naked, but I did like the fact that Denti had to sleep next to him. It was funny to hear stories about Denti waking up to an eyeful of Proust's ass.

The dirt on him concerns raunchy e-mails he sent his girlfriend, Clementine. She's twenty-seven and a staff sergeant in charge of the supply section for our unit. She's about 5'8" with washboard abs, dark Portuguese skin, and size D fake breasts that her ex-boyfriend bought her. For reasons unbeknownst to any of us, nobody in the command (especially First Sergeant Mardine) likes Proust or Clementine, and the second it was found out that they were a couple, they were forbidden from seeing each other and put on separate shifts so that one would be sleeping while the other worked.

Long story short, Proust and Clementine couldn't see each other so they e-mailed each other really raunchy, nasty messages. This girl Consuela, who works in supply with Clementine, hates her because Clementine wants Consuela's job. Clementine works late one night and reads the e-mails from Proust. She gets horny and decides to "take care of herself" in the bathroom. While she's there, Consuela walks in and sees the computer on. Proust's e-mail is still on the screen, so she prints off twenty copies of this completely raunchy e-mail. I mean, Proust was talking about all the toys he wants to use on her and vice versa. Around midnight, Consuela takes the copies of the e-mail and tapes them to the back of all the bathroom doors—male and female.

First Sergeant Mardine sees the papers on the doors and orders someone to take them down. Consuela is sent down south, and Clementine is fired from being in charge of supply. She is now First Sergeant Mardine's assistant so that she can "keep an eye on her."

✛

Thankfully Proust is alone and not with his significant other, Clementine. Ever since the two of them got in trouble for that e-mail incident a few months back they've been trying to hang low and stay under the radar.

"You guys have got to come see this," Proust yells over to Reto as I take my at-bat.

"What it's about?" I yell as I swing and miss.

"You guys have just got to see it," Proust says, backing away from my batter's box.

I put the broom handle bat down and we follow him into the ER.

"I was randomly looking through our paging logs and I found some interesting pages between certain people in our unit. Since you guys are the only ones on shift that I like, I figured I'd show you," Proust says as he sits behind a computer screen.

Certain people throughout the hospital have pagers, and the paging log is a computer program that everyone has to log into if they want to page someone.

"I was just randomly playing with the computer and then I found that there is a log of every page ever sent to anyone within the system."

Proust starts naming eight people that are having affairs and shows us all the pages with the texts being sent back and forth between them.

I miss you baby.

Meet me by the bathrooms.

I'm thinking about last night big boy.

I'm wearing your panties you left at my place.

Reto and I go through all the pages with Proust, but it's not that impressive; we already knew all these people were having affairs.

"That's just the tip of the iceberg. Here's yesterday's pages between Staff Sergeant Blett, she's married to a man back home, and Chief Ward Master Pyne, who is also married to someone back home."

I found someone to cover guard duty for you. Come straight to my office when they get there.

"That son of a bitch!" I yell at the computer.

Reto and Proust look at me and I point to the screen.

"I'm the person he's talking about. I'm the guard they sent so they could get it on."

'Thank you so much for this,' Blett said to me, and then she runs into Chief Ward Master Pyne's office. Forty-five minutes later, she comes out putting all of her gear back on and tightening her belt."

✚

Later I go into the bathroom and take half of a pill out of my pocket. Denti went to a doctor a week ago and told him he was having problems with his back. The doctor gave him a prescription for Percocet, and Denti then sold me some of the pills at five dollars apiece. I usually only take half a pill at a time, partly because I don't want to get too messed up in case something important happens and partly because the pills cost five bucks a pop. I take them because I know I shouldn't be taking them, but they make me feel good. I don't have to deal with the pain and . . . I know that it can be harmful, but . . . it helps me forget that this is the Army and a high-ranking sergeant made me do extra guard duty just so she could have an adulterous quickie.

WEEK 2, DAY 3, IRAQ

2200 HOURS, OR

"Soldiers keep disappearing and no one says anything about it. One day they're here and the next day they're gone, and it only happens to the female soldiers."

Hudge is on the computer sending an e-mail to her mom; she doesn't look up as she speaks.

"They're all pregnant, silly."

"So you're telling me that all these girls have gotten pregnant here in Iraq?"

"I think one of the three has a husband and was trying to get pregnant while on leave. The other two haven't been on leave, yet, have husbands back home, but got pregnant here," says Hudge.

The whole situation is like the reversal of the old milkman story from World War II. All the men are off fighting the war and the women at home get lonely, and some of them sleep with the milkman. Then the men come home and there's a little baby waiting in their house. The wife tells him that someone just left the baby on their doorstep. Meanwhile, the baby grows up to look an awful lot like the milkman. In Iraq and in our unit it's the reverse. The men stayed home, and while the women are away they get pregnant.

WEEK 3, DAY 4, IRAQ

0100 HOURS, MY ROOM

The pins-and-needles feeling you get when your hand or foot falls asleep is now vibrating throughout my entire body. My body feels numb, yet I feel as though every inch of my body is being poked with a needle. I feel as if I am the static on a television screen.

I took one-and-a-half Percocets, the last of the pills that Denti sold me. I also took one sleeping pill and smoked three Camel Light cigarettes.

I can feel all the different substances working at once. The sleeping pill is making my mind hazy, the Percocet is combining with the sleeping pills and giving me the reverberations, and the nicotine is what's keeping me awake. As my mind drifts off from the pills, I can feel the nicotine coursing through my veins. It's like giving my mind the equivalent of a B_{12} shot. I still can't move my body, but my mind is awake and aware. It wants to sleep but it can't.

I hear shouting outside. The base military police must be doing surprise room inspections. A few days ago, two Marines were doing a search of houses in a nearby Iraqi town and they came across a stash of dozens of pounds of marijuana. One of them grabbed a handful and took it back to the base with him. Somehow he got caught, and now the military police are conducting random checks. They're using one of the dogs from the K-9 unit to sniff out the drugs. It's actually a bomb-sniffing dog, but, hey, leave it to the Army to reclassify someone.

WEEK 4, DAY 1, IRAQ

2000 HOURS, OR

"Hey, man. I was wondering if you've got any Percocets or Vicodins?" I ask Proust as I look around, making sure that no one's watching. Denti's prescription ran out, and he told me that Proust has one for Vicodin and that he sells his pills, too.

"Not right now, man. I sold them all. Two more weeks. Why don't you try Robo tripping or Coricidin tripping?"

I stand there and consider Proust's advice, but I let the thought fade out of my mind as I remember all the people I've known who've done one or the other. Robo tripping is when you down a bottle of Robitussin as quickly as possible. It's supposed to give you a trip similar to an acid trip. When I was in San Antonio doing my initial training to become an operating room medic, there were too many people that got sent to the ER from overdosing to make me ever want to do it. But in San Antonio there were twice as many people who would go Coricidin tripping. Coricidin is a cough and cold medicine for people with high blood pressure. If you take ten to thirteen pills, you will feel as though you are in a cartoon. But if you take too many, your life will permanently feel that way. I've heard countless stories of people who have gone insane after Coricidin tripping one too many times.

"Nah, that's cool, man. I just want to forget some things; I don't feel like going retarded. I'll just come back in two weeks."

WEEK 4, DAY 6, IRAQ

0910 HOURS, CHURCH

There aren't many people here, maybe thirty, and they're all taking up the first three rows or so on either side of the aisle. Just like in school, I'm in the back where it's easier to avoid eye contact.

✚

At first I was hesitant to go; it's been a while since I've gone to church. I was raised Catholic, but ever since I left home at eighteen I haven't really gone to church. I know that going now couldn't hurt. Besides, it's getting too expensive to pay five dollars a pill, and I need something to take the edge off.

The choir is getting up to sing. It's Captain Tarr, Colonel Reke, another woman, and Reto. I'm staring at Captain Tarr as I try and let her voice penetrate my soul. Her face shines brightly and her lips are rosy red, but the comfort of the song leaves me. I can only think about how in a few hours those lips will be wrapped around the penile shaft of some civilian contractor, like the time I saw her. In the dining facility, I hear all the Marines calling her "The Viper" because she pounces on all the guys she sees. Sixty years old and she's singing "praise be to God." A few hours later her mouth will be muffled by some anonymous dick, and a few hours after that she'll most likely call home and tell her kids how much she loves them.

MONTH 9

"WHEN I CLOSE MY EYES I DREAM OF DEATH AND WAR. WHEN I OPEN MY EYES I SEE DEATH AND WAR. . . ."

WEEK 1, DAY 2, IRAQ

0100 HOURS, MY ROOM

Torres saw his first patient die today, and he told me the entire story. The patient had an open chest wound. He was losing blood as fast as they could put it back in. The doctor was a general surgeon attempting open heart surgery. Normally this would never be done; a procedure like that would happen in a controlled setting by a trained heart doctor. We have no choice, though, because the Army isn't full of doctors. We often don't have the time or resources to send every patient to a specialist; we've got to make do with whom and what we have. Often we have doctors going above and beyond their scope of practice. We have podiatrists and urologists doing the work of a general surgeon while a general surgeon does the work of a vascular or heart specialist.

The diaphragm of the patient is cut and Torres can see the heart as it beats up and down, up and down, squirting blood out with each beat of the heart. Slowly the blood becomes less, not because the doctors are stopping the bleeding, but because the man is running out of blood. Torres is standing there with his feet deep in an inch of blood. The heart goes up to beat then back down, and it stays down. The anesthesia machine beeps, and the doctor throws down the instrument that was in his hand.

"Damn it, time of death 11:15."

WEEK 1, DAY 7, IRAQ

0400 HOURS, MY ROOM

I walk into the hospital and immediately notice the familiar smell of ether in the air. With the hospital's whitewashed walls and the soldiers walking around in a tired daze, I feel as if I'm in an insane asylum. I notice a trail of blood in front of me and my curiosity overrides my diligence of being on time to work. I sling my rifle over my shoulder and begin to follow the trail, keeping my head down and avoiding eye contact with all the tired eyes. The trail ends with a patient sitting outside of the ER. I look up and see the faded eyes of a boy in uniform, someone hurting and looking for help. I realize that it's me and I stare into my own eyes.

0405 HOURS, MY ROOM

Waking up in bed I become disoriented.

The dreams are becoming more vivid every night. I read books on dream interpretation. I read books on Freud. I look for answers in my dreams and I find nothing. I spend my days walking around in a tired daze, and I spend my nights tossing and turning as I run through the dream world. Am I awake or dreaming? It doesn't matter anymore. When I close my eyes I dream of death and war. When I open my eyes I see death and war. I blink and as my eyes close I see images of death, and as they flutter open I see death— there is no escaping it. It's said that the second we are born we start to die. The exact second that we as humans come alive we start to die. The choice is ours what we do with our life, but the story ultimately ends the same for everyone.

1500 HOURS, OR

"You've got to do it for us. We can't take it anymore. None of us can. And we know you can't either." Reto, Denti, Chandler, Torres, and I are all surrounding Sergeant Hudge. We are voicing our complaints and asking her to bring them up with Sergeant Gagney and Colonel Reke. Once again Gagney is treating us like crap. His constant yelling and verbal abuse are actually getting worse, he's actually inhibiting our jobs more than helping.

"What do you want me to do?" Hudge yells back. "We've already had meetings with the chief ward masters and nothing happened. He won't tell us when the climate control meetings are, so we can't complain. Last time I tried this, they called me insane."

"That's exactly why we need to do something about him," says Reto.

"Maybe if we just talk to him one more time," says Chandler.

"Tell him he doesn't even need to come into work, that we can work better without him," I say.

"Listen guys, I've got the answer . . ." Denti begins, as he picks up a can of coffee from the break room table and holds it in the air. "Let's just put something in his drink, like a laxative or something. Then we can take the toilet paper out of all the bathrooms."

Torres, Reto, and I look at each other. We nod in agreement.

"Not a bad idea Denti, not bad at all. Won't solve our problems, but I'm sure as hell that it will feel good to watch him clutch his stomach as he runs toward the bathroom." I begin to laugh as I speak. "Haha. I wonder what the hell he would actually use for toilet paper."

"All right. All right," Hudge says, putting her hands in the air. "I don't want to hear anymore. Don't put anything in his drink, at least not yet. I will try talking to him and we'll see what happens."

"Thanks," Reto says, putting his hand on her shoulder. "And remember, if anything happens you've got all of us backing you. The Army will have to do something. . . ."

WEEK 2, DAY 1, IRAQ

1500 HOURS, OR

"Excuse me, Sergeant Gagney, can I speak to you for a moment?" Hudge approaches Gagney at his desk. He is playing *World of Warcraft* on his computer, and Reto and I are in the corner of the room pretending to play Rummy 500 and watching the interaction.

"What is it about?" Gagney sternly makes even his question sound like an authoritative statement.

"I was hoping I could talk to you in private about an issue."

"God. What is it with you people? Fine!" Gagney flips his computer screen down and stands up. Hudge walks into one of the rooms that we use as a changing room and Gagney follows, slamming the door behind him.

"Let's do it." Reto and I head to the door to try to listen to the muffled conversation.

"NO ONE likes you. None of these complaints are real. They're all lying to you. They bitch to me about you behind your back," Gagney says.

"Listen, they all came to me yesterday and complained. It's not me, everyone is—"

"SHUT UP. You're lying. No one came to you yesterday, and no one is complaining about me. You really are crazy. The mental health officer and the chaplain were right; you have problems. And you're nothing more than a dumb bitch."

"Don't tell me to shut up," her voice is crackling as she speaks. "You're a terrible leader. And you need to change or we're going to do something about it." Hudge's voice whimpers out.

Gagney starts laughing; it sounds challenging.

"And what the hell do you think you're going to do? I'm putting Cather in charge. And you know what? If you or anyone else has a problem with me, you can take it up with the chief ward masters. That's what they're here for."

Reto and I look at each other at the mention of Cather. Cather, the fifty-eight-year-old specialist who replaced Crade, has kept true to his word, and all this time he has yet to do any further surgeries. In fact, no one knows what he really does all day; he's gone most of the time.

"Fine! I will see the chief ward masters." Reto and I hear Hudge yell. Her voice has a newfound confidence to it.

A door slams shut. It's the other entrance to the room that Gagney and Hudge are in. Hudge walks out. Her eyes are red and she laughs as she sees Reto and me standing there pretending as if we weren't listening.

"It didn't go like I expected. Tomorrow at 1400 hours I'm going to try and see the chief ward masters, and we'll take it from there."

WEEK 2, DAY 3, IRAQ

0830 HOURS, OR

The song "Bother" by Stone Sour is playing in the background. I made a special playlist specifically for when I work with Dr. Bill. It is a combination of classical music for him and alternative rock for me.

"Cauterize the skin here for me, will you?"

The patient is a British soldier, and he has a wound to his leg. We are stopping the bleeding and putting his leg back together.

"Have you heard about that surgeon in our southern hospital, the one who molested those two female patients?" Dr. Bill asks me while tying a knot around one of our patient's veins.

"Yeah."

"Well, he was in the paper today. His punishment came down. He's only getting a fine of $12,000 and a forty-five-day suspension. He molested two girls and he gets a fine and forty-five days of vacation." Dr. Bill throws the scissors in his hands to the ground.

He's been agitated about more as well. He's heard the truth about why so many of the Iraqi patients we've done surgery on have died. After we saved their lives, they would be shipped to Iraqi hospitals. Once there, one of three things would happen:

1. The Iraqi hospital wouldn't have any of the proper supplies and the patient would end up dying.

2. Patients of one religion would be killed because they were sent to a hospital in an area where a different religion is predominant.

3. We send the patients to a hospital and insurgents come in and kill them for being seen by an American doctor.

"Get me a new pair of scissors," Bill yells at the nurse.

1330 HOURS, OR

Gagney's got something up his sleeve.

"Anthony, page Sergeant Hudge and tell her to be here at 1400."

Gagney is calm, almost happy. He's been missing all day.

I page Hudge, telling her to be in here at 1400 hours. When I get back Gagney is sitting down, filling in some military forms.

1355 HOURS, OR

"Sergeant Hudge, glad to see you. Please follow me."

Gagney turns and walks into the room where he and Hudge had the argument yesterday. Reto's not on shift yet, but I'm listening to them.

"Here you go, Sergeant Hudge. I've just made these counseling forms. Please sign and date them."

"You can't give me three of these."

"I'd like you to sign them."

"I'm not signing anything. . . ."

Counseling statements are the civilian equivalent of performance evaluations. They're supposed to be done once a month and you can either have a good one or a bad one. However, if you get three bad ones in a row (supposed to be months apart, not minutes), it's grounds for loss of pay.

Gagney starts yelling something, but I jump back from the door as I hear footsteps coming down the hall. Colonel Reke walks in the room, grabs a can of soda, and walks back out. I head back toward the door. It's silent inside—this isn't good. Ten minutes go by and I knock on the door—no one answers. I open the door and no one's inside. They must have gone out the side door.

1425 HOURS, OR

"I don't know what to say. The man will do whatever it takes to keep his position," Hudge says as she walks in the door. Reto and I are sitting down in the break room.

"He's like an alligator: He doesn't do anything all day and saves his energy only to hunt his prey and bite their heads off. Meanwhile, I get irritable bowel syndrome. I did tell him to fuck off and left to go talk to one of the chief ward masters. When I get there, Pyne was the only one there. Gagney follows behind me, slamming the door shut as he does. As soon as the door is closed he starts verbally attacking me. I try to defend myself, but Pyne says I'm just saying it as retribution for the counseling statements that Gagney gave me—but I hadn't mentioned the counseling statements so he must have already known Gagney was going to give them to me. I couldn't talk about it anymore, we'd been talking for ten minutes, it was already planned—I've officially been relieved of my position as second shift leader."

WEEK 2, DAY 7, IRAQ

1300 HOURS, OR

Here's what my days are like: I wake up in the morning and smoke to get rid of my headache, then I walk to work, in a hundred and twenty degrees of heat, and then spend all day covered in blood. Then I go home, take some pills, and fall asleep. It's as if everything is piling up, and after trying to make myself dead to emotions for so long, they're finally starting to catch up and I don't know what do with them.

"How are you feeling Anthony, are you all right? You look worn down." Gagney looks at me and puts his hand on my shoulder. We make eye contact for the first time in months.

"I'll be fine . . . thanks," I say to Gagney.

"If you need anything, or ever need to talk, you can talk to me."

I don't know whether it's because I've been filled with such emotion lately, but hearing Gagney say this makes me want to forget every nasty thing he's ever done.

"Yeah I know, thanks," I reply.

Gagney turns and leaves while I am left here in shock.

I want to continue to hate Gagney; it's all I know and I'm good at it. I've grown accustomed to my hate—it's comfortable, it's my friend, and it's always there for me. But now it feels as though it's slowly leaving, and I'm not sure I want it to leave because I'm afraid of what I'll be left with.

I am reminded of a story I once heard about the explorer Marco Polo. Whenever he was going on an expedition he would take a team of people with him, and in this team he would always bring one person that everyone disliked or hated. They said it gave everyone else in the group a common enemy and a way to relate to each other, a way to get all their anger off of each other and off of the conditions and channel all of it toward one person. I now feel like I lost that one person, but everyone else still has him so now I'm the outsider.

Denti is sitting in the break room eating potato chips and drinking orange soda. He complains about some floor cleaning job Gagney had given him and I already feel like an outsider.

Gagney walks in as Denti is telling me about the floor mopping assignment.

"Damn it, Denti! I told you to go mop the floor an hour ago," Gagney says then looks at me. "And look at you. You were there when I told him; you were going to just let him sit here stuffing his fat mouth with chips and soda instead of moping the floor! Now both of you can stay here an extra hour and mop the entire OR. All the rooms!"

Denti and I look at each other. We're connecting again. I can feel my anger and hate coming back as his anger also rises. I feel relieved; my old friend is back. Even though he'd only been gone for a few minutes, it still felt good to have him back. Gagney storms out of the room, but before he does he gives me a look. Denti and I spend the next hour mopping the floor and complaining about Gagney.

Second shift comes in, and even though they don't help us with mopping the floor, they do join in the complaining about Gagney. All of us standing around there, making fun of Gagney, having a good time. I think about all the times we all stood around like this laughing and cracking jokes and how it has helped us bond. Maybe Marco Polo was onto something, maybe even Gagney is onto something.

WEEK 3, DAY 4, IRAQ

2000 HOURS, SLEEPING AREA

Proust picks up a plastic bag filled with chopped up green leaves.

"Hey Johnson, tell Anthony the story you just told me."

"I don't feel like it," Johnson yells back and lies down in bed.

"He just fucked one of the interpreters," Proust says. "He fucked the big girl, the one with the big hips and nice ass. He just found out she's a prostitute, too, and people on base have been paying her hundreds of dollars to sleep with her." Proust laughs. "Now he's worried that he might have an STD or something."

"Shut UP!" Johnson yells, throwing a pillow at Proust.

Proust ignores it and looks at me.

"You ever heard of *Salvia divinorum*?"

"Sounds familiar."

"It's a totally legal drug. Native Americans use it in some type of shaman rituals so the government can't outlaw it."

Proust goes on to tell me that salvia is comparable to LSD in the type of high it gives you. He explains that several people from the ER have ordered it online and are smoking it.

"Take some so you can meet your spirit animal," he says.

The thought of soldiers with an M-16 and three hundred rounds of ammo, tripping on a drug that makes them talk to spirit animals. . . . I get up and leave, telling Proust I'll be back in a few days for more Vicodin or Percocet.

WEEK 4, DAY 6, IRAQ

0100 HOURS, MY ROOM

As I lay in bed, staring at my computer and browsing the web, I come across a quote: "Not all scars show, not all wounds heal. Sometimes you can't always see the pain someone feels."

It makes me think about our hospital and what we're doing here. The real wounds of this war are going to be the ones that we can't fix, the ones that our medical equipment and training have nothing to do with. The Iraqi child growing up without a mother or father, the Iraqi widowed husband or wife, the American child growing up without a mother or father, the American widowed husband or wife—these are the real wounds of the war. These are the ones we can't heal. Everyone in our hospital is going through their own things. We are not just fighting this war in Iraq; we are fighting it within ourselves.

We are a hospital, but I think we're working on the wrong wounds. I don't think we can heal the wounds of war with mere medical care. I think about the speech my drill sergeant once gave when I was in basic training. I now understand what he was talking about. *"And for the real unlucky ones, you will come home so emotionally disfigured that you wish you had died over there."*

We are going to leave Iraq, and since we're not an infantry unit, most likely all of us are going to get home safe and sound without any physical injuries. I doubt that any of us will be so overwhelmed that we'll wish we had died. But I feel a pang of emotional shrapnel as I watch the countless number of husbands and wives having affairs. The war goes on. Crade looks for a way out of his pain and twice he finds suicide attempts as the answer. The GOBs then had a decision to make—what to do, what not to do—and they did nothing. The war goes on. Specialist Meade, Captain Tarr, Lieutenant Hamilton, and countless more—all of them looking to fill this hole they feel in themselves, and they choose anonymous sex to fill it. The war goes on. Sergeant Hudge and Staff Sergeant Gagney and all of us have to deal with our own blood, our own lives, our own anger, and each other. The war goes on.

MONTH 10

"IF SOMEONE FEELS AN EMOTION BUT DOESN'T ALLOW THEMSELVES TO EXPRESS IT, WHERE DOES IT GO?"

WEEK 1, DAY 5, IRAQ

1600 HOURS, OR

"Ladies and gentlemen, let's give a big round of applause for Colonel Jelly," one of the GOBs says. The GOBs and Colonel Jelly are holding an award ceremony for themselves and some of the doctors. The MDs have only been with us for three months, but they're getting awards.

"You've got to help our buddy out. He's hurt very badly. We went to the ER, but the doors are locked," two Marines say to a specialist in the ICW as they hold their friend and fellow Marine up and place him in a nearby chair. A specialist, Linhorst, a medic who works in the ICW looks at the patient: young, twenty years old, holding his mouth and jaw. Linhorst looks at the two Marines that brought him in.

"What happened to him?"

"We were working on a machine when part of it combusted."

"He's an engineer?"

"He passed out for a second, and when he came to he was crying from the pain but he couldn't talk. Then the ER was locked." The Marine looks around. "I mean, the only person we saw. . . ."

"I'll see what I can do," Linhorst says as he turns and heads toward the ER.

"Excuse me, sergeant," Linhorst whispers as he touches Staff Sergeant Blett's shoulder. "We have a patient that needs to be seen."

Blett turns partially around, only exposing one cheek to Linhorst. "What's wrong with him? Is he awake? I didn't hear the chopper land."

"I'm not sure what his injury is. He's holding his mouth and his friends brought him in."

"I'll see him after the ceremony," Blett says as she turns her head back around, hoping that maybe one of the awards is for her.

Linhorst turns and walks back to the ICW. The soldier is still holding his mouth, and tears are running down his cheeks.

"She said she'll be here as quick as she can."

Linhorst looks at the patient, though, and he can tell something is wrong. Marines are trained to deal with all types of pain, but this soldier is screaming, he is screaming through his eyes.

1617 HOURS, OR

"Where the hell is everyone? This is a hospital." One of the Marines is beginning to get frantic; his friend hasn't been seen by anyone besides Specialist Linhorst.

Linhorst turns again and goes back toward the ER.

Colonel Jelly is still giving out awards and congratulating another one of the GOBs.

"Sergeant," Linhorst whispers to Blett again. "I really think you should come look at this patient."

Blett turns around and lets out a sigh saying, "Fine."

"What seems to be the problem?" Blett asks, looking at the Marine in the chair, totally forgetting that his injury is in his mouth.

"It's about time. I think his jaw might be broken or something," one of the Marines jumps in.

"Well, if that's the case there's nothing I can do. You'll have to wait for a doctor," Blett says as she turns and walks back toward the ceremony.

1634 HOURS, OR

"Where's my soldier?" the Marine colonel says as he comes barreling into the ICW. "And where the hell is everyone in this damn hospital?"

The Marines promptly straighten their backs and stand at the position of attention; the injured one stays seated.

"Sir," one Marine begins "Corporal Ellenberg is the injured one. His jaw is injured, maybe broken."

"Broken? Well, what did the doctor have to say?"

"Sir. The doctors haven't seen him yet."

"Marine, what the hell do you mean he hasn't been seen yet? I got the call twenty minutes ago about the injury. How long have you been here?"

"Sir. We have been here . . ." the Marine looks down at his watch, "a little over a half-hour."

The Marine colonel turns and looks at Linhorst. "Where the hell is the doctor, and why hasn't my Marine been seen in a half-hour?"

"Sir. Our doctors are all at a ceremony in the ER. I got my section leader, Sergeant Blett, but she went back to the ceremony. She said he needed to wait to see a doctor."

"Well, soldier, I want a doctor to look at my Marine and I want them to do it now! No section leader, I want a damn! doctor. I mean this is a hospital, isn't it?"

"Yes, sir," Linhorst says as he turns around and heads toward the ER. The Marine colonel follows him.

"Excuse me, sir," Linhorst whispers, tapping on the shoulder of one of the ER doctors.

"What is it, soldier?" the doctor replies, unable to take his eyes off of Colonel Jelly, who is once again standing in front of the crowd of people.

"Sir, we have a patient that's waiting in the. . . ."

"Soldier, is the patient walking? Did he get he brought in by a helicopter?"

"Well, no sir, but. . . ."

"Is he bleeding anywhere?"

"No, sir, but. . . ."

"I'll tell you what. I'll see him right after this. . . ."

The doctor then walks toward the stage with five other doctors as Colonel Jelly announces they'll all be getting awards for their great medical care.

Linhorst looks at the Marine colonel, and the colonel looks back; neither knows what to do.

1646 HOURS, OR

The ER doctor, whom Linhorst was talking to, finishes up giving a speech on giving good medical care and then walks back toward Linhorst and the Marine colonel.

"There, now was that so bad? Let's go see this patient," the doctor says to Linhorst as he turns and walks toward the ICW.

WEEK 1, DAY 6, IRAQ

0730 HOURS, OR

"Anthony, you're in the case with me today," Dr. Bill yells toward me. "We have a long case ahead of us. A Marine came in

yesterday and his whole jaw is broken. We've got to rewire it. Did
you bring your iPod?"

WEEK 2, DAY 4, IRAQ

2350 HOURS, MY ROOM

The new unit will replace us in about two more months. It
means we have to start going through a process called out-
processing. We have mental health tests done to see if any of us
have PTSD (post-traumatic stress disorder) and get tested for all
types of diseases that we could have got caught in-country.

"Ten months of everyone having sex with random people and
now they finally decide it's time to check if they have any STDs,"
Markham announces as he opens the door to our room. Reto,
Denti, and I are watching a bootleg copy of the movie *Superbad*.

"I'm late getting out of work because we're doing everyone's
damn STD tests and we're told not to put any of it on the damn
books."

"So how many confirmed?" Reto asks, not expecting a real
answer.

"Only two so far, and you know what—Meade is totally free
and clear."

It's sad to hear about people and the circumstances that they'll
have to deal with, all for making one bad decision. But Meade
being clean? Reto reaches over onto my computer and pauses the
movie.

"She should get checked again. Porpe was in my room the other day. She says she needs a place to hang out for a few hours. I ask her what's going on and she tells me that Meade is in her room getting gangbanged by three different Marines."

I wish I could just forget everything and go back to thinking that everyone in the military is an American hero. I wish I still had someone to look up to, although I know it's impossible. None of it seems to make sense, and I can't understand how people can do what they do.

WEEK 3, DAY 6, IRAQ

0200 HOURS, MY ROOM

I wonder if someone feels an emotion but doesn't allow himself to express it . . . well, where does it go? If one man gives another man a present but the other man doesn't accept it, who does it belong to? If our mind, body, and heart send a message of what we're feeling but we refuse to accept it, where does it go? Bottled up until you become emotionally constipated? Some people become depressive, abusive, stressed, or destructive, and some people develop PTSD.

I've only cried six times in my life. We're warriors on the battlefield but cowards in our own minds and hearts. When something bad happens we retreat into our shells like scared turtles. We allow ourselves to become prisoners of our own walls, of our own making. Everything in life consists of cause and effect, yet often we refuse to acknowledge one or the other.

I am lying in bed crying, and it's probably going to save me from getting PTSD. When you push things down so far for so long and then finally let them go, they all come rushing out, and instead of being able to deal with things one at a time, you're forced to deal with things all at once. Some wait too long and can't handle the outpouring.

That's actually what I believe happened to Crade and why he tried to kill himself. When it happens, your mind goes blank, your body takes over, and you start to cry and your body begins to convulse as if looking for an exit for all the emotion. I keep crying into my pillow for I don't know how long. My mind slowly fades back. I stop and regain composure over myself. The first thing I think is: "Damn, I hope none of my roommates heard that." I look around and they're all sleeping or at least pretending to be asleep. It's an absurd thought, and I begin chuckling. That I could have such a cathartic experience and the first thing I would think would be "I hope no one heard me." I laugh at myself and it feels good, like it's coming from my core. I feel relieved. I feel as if an emotional weight had been lifted off my shoulders—twenty pounds death, twenty pounds hate, and ten pounds sadness. I feel like I do at the gym, knowing that from carrying all the weight I am now stronger for the next time. Then it starts again. More weight will pile on as I either accept or neglect feelings and thoughts. I can't cry anymore. For now it's all gone. It hit me as quick as a tsunami and left just as quickly.

WEEK 4, DAY 2, IRAQ

1000 HOURS, DOCTOR'S OFFICE

"Yes, sir, I'm having problems sleeping."

"All right, soldier. I'm going to write you a prescription for Ambien."

Melatonin takes too long, and I have to take too many pills to fall asleep, other pills aren't effective, Benadryl leaves me restless, and NyQuil leaves me drowsy the next day. The majority of our hospital is taking some type of sleep medication. Some take melatonin and some take NyQuil or something similar, and some people take a sleep medication called Ambien. Ambien is a powerful sleep medication, and it's easy to become addicted to it. If you take it one night then you can't sleep the next night, so you need to constantly take it. A lot of people in the unit are taking it and they swear by it. Proust tells me that if I take one of the pills and don't sleep, I will have trippy, yet awesome, hallucinations. At first I am hesitant. It could be more than I can handle. It could turn bad. Fuck it; I've got a prescription and it's free—which sounds better than paying five dollars a pill for Vicodin and Percocet.

MONTH 11

"I'VE SURVIVED ALL OF THIS, BUT I'M STILL AFRAID TO GO BACK TO THE REAL WORLD."

WEEK 1, DAY 4, IRAQ

2305 HOURS, MY ROOM

Reto is holding his computer with a shit-eating grin on his face.

"What is it, man, I was just about to go to sleep?"

Reto walks over and sits down on the bed next to me; I sit up and look at his computer screen. There's an image of Staff Sergeant Clementine naked and shoving a dildo into her ass.

"Wwooooah!" I say, staring at the picture and trying to take my eyes away at the same time.

"Someone asked Proust if they could copy some of the music from his computer and Proust said sure. But instead of copying just the music, they copied all the media files, including, music, videos, and pictures."

Reto begins flipping through the pictures on his computer. They all consist of Clementine naked and shoving different adult toys into different holes; sometimes one at a time, sometimes two. Reto's slideshow ends with Clementine shoving almost her entire fist into her vagina.

"Everyone has the pictures now. Everyone just keeps sending them to everyone."

Chandler walks in holding his computer and a can of Pepsi.

"Damn it, Reto beat me to it."

WEEK 2, DAY 3, IRAQ

1440 HOURS, OUTSIDE THE HOSPITAL

I'm signed up for extra duty detail. Thanks, Gagney.

"It starts at 1500 hours so leave now. You'll be filling sandbags behind the ER."

I grab my coat and head behind the ER. There is a crew of six filling sandbags: three men holding the bags and three shoveling the sand in. Staff Sergeant Clementine is in charge of the detail, watching over everyone and making sure the sand goes properly in the bag.

"Soldier, you're late!" Staff Sergeant Clementine says to me as I pick up a shovel. "This detail started at 1430. Why are you late?"

I drop the shovel and stand at the position of parade rest, hands behind my back, legs shoulder-width apart.

"Sergeant, I was told the detail didn't start until 1500."

Staff Sergeant Clementine starts to yell at me, and all I can see in my mind are the pictures Reto showed me. Clementine yells, and I see her trying to bite her own nipple. As she switches her weight from one leg to the other, I see a pink dildo penetrating her from behind. After a few minutes of this, she thinks I've had enough and then tells me to get to work. I need a cigarette.

WEEK 2, DAY 7, IRAQ

1330 HOURS, OR

A man has certain urges: The first one is to procreate and thus create something. The second is to fight or destroy something. The third one is probably some esoteric self-actualization, but I've never gotten that far so I have no idea what the third one is.

Mixed martial arts, Ultimate Fighting, and other blood sports are on the rise again. During the time of Roman rule, tens of thousand of people would load into the Collosseum to watch men fight each other to the death or get mauled by lions. That was thousands of years ago, and here we are today with the same hobbies. The only difference is now people don't fight to the death, just to the knowledge that one indeed could kill one's opponent if he doesn't pass out or tap out.

Boxing matches: 2000 Hours the sign reads as Reto and I open the door to the hospital. Our unit is going to have a sponsored boxing match for anyone willing to fight.

2001 HOURS, BOXING ARENA

"Ladies and gentlemen, and Marines, welcome to our boxing event. . . ."

Two men enter the ring. It's the lower weight class, and the two fighters look like they might weigh two hundred pounds combined. They step into the ring, and their little fists of fury begin to pound one another.

2200 HOURS, BOXING ARENA

We've never had more fun in Iraq. Everyone is cheering. All it took for us to have a good time were hot dogs, hamburgers, and two men in a ring beating the shit out of each other. The boxing event even has ring girls (clothed) that the guys can holler at, and the women don't seem to mind because they all scream as the men come out of their corners, shirts off, sweating, bleeding, fighting hard. I'm not certain why everyone else enjoyed it, but I can say why I did: Watching two men enter a ring for no other purpose but to compete against each other and give 100 percent of themselves, knowing that there will only be one winner and one loser, is primal and cathartic.

WEEK 3, DAY 4, IRAQ

1330 HOURS, OUTSIDE THE HOSPITAL

"Anthony. . . ." I hear someone yell my name. It's Sergeant Cardoza, Torres's girlfriend and my fifth roommate.

"What's up?" I yell back.

"Do you remember when you were in the bunker during the mortar attack for the incident you got your CAB?" I pause for a second as if I truly might not be able to remember a time I was almost killed.

"Yeah, I remember it."

"OK, good. Now in the bunker with you. . . . I know it was you, Staff Sergeant Elwood, and Specialist Boredo. . . . but was there anyone else in the bunker?"

"No."

"Are you sure there was no one else in the bunker. . . . ?"

"What? No. Why?" I ask, confused. I'm not sure if I understand what Cardoza is asking. I'm not sure if she wants me to say something like God was in the bunker with me.

"Wasn't Specialist Bane in there with you?"

Boredo's girlfriend? "Cardoza, what the hell are you talking about? No, she wasn't in there with us," I reply.

"Are you sure?"

It's been several months since the attack, but I can still see all the details in my mind, and besides, they have my written story. . . .

"Yes, I'm sure she wasn't there. I'm one hundred percent positive she wasn't. Why? What's going on?"

Cardoza looks over both her shoulders, grabs me by the arm, and takes me to the corner of a building.

"Specialist Bane . . ." Cardoza begins as she once again looks over both her shoulders. "She is saying that she was in the bunker with you, Elwood, and Boredo when the attack happened, and now she's filling out paperwork so that she can get a Combat Action Badge as well. Boredo has changed his story and said that she was there. I talked to Elwood, too, and he said he doesn't care; he'll go along with whatever."

Unbelievable.

"I'm not telling you to do it, Anthony. Personally I wouldn't do it."

"Absolutely, unequivocally, NO, I won't do it. These fucking people tried to not include me in their stories and now they want me to lie so that Boredo's girlfriend can get an award," I say, disgusted.

I know it's not Cardoza's doing, but I don't feel like looking at her anymore. I don't feel like looking at anyone.

I am unable to comprehend how people would give up their integrity and self-respect just to receive an award.

All I can think about is a quote I once heard by Napoleon: "A man will fight long and hard for a bit of colored ribbon."

WEEK 4, DAY 5, IRAQ

0100 HOURS, MY ROOM

I'm laying in bed and my eyes are wide open. I can't sleep; the Ambien isn't working. I'm not hallucinating or seeing things, and I'm not falling asleep. My mind is too wired. I'm scared. I'm really scared. More scared than thinking I might go to jail, more scared than all the nights I spent hunched over in a bunker as mortars landed all around me.

I'm scared about the future. What happens when I get home? I'm twenty-one, and I don't know what I want in life. Sure, I can go back to college, but that's only delaying the inevitable. I think about all the people in my unit. I see people who are respected in society. They're doctors, nurses, pharmacists, anesthesiologists, and since we're reservists some of them also have different jobs in the civilian world. They're police officers, teachers, and firefighters. But they don't have respect for themselves and one another. I'm scared because I don't want to end up like any of these people, and I really don't know how to prevent it. I remember someone once telling me something about finding a mentor or finding someone that has what I want in life and then modeling that person's behaviors and attitudes. I tried finding someone; I really did. But I couldn't find a single person in my unit that had what I wanted. I'm appalled by the majority of them. But I'm no better than them, I know that.

I'm twenty-one years old and I have lived on my own since I was eighteen. During surgical training I assisted in delivering almost a dozen babies. I left home to go to war. I've seen people die and grown men cry. I've cowered in a bunker for hours at a time, fearing for my life. I've gone days without sleep and have assisted in hundreds of surgeries. I've survived all of this, but I'm still afraid to go back to the real world. In the Army and in Iraq I don't have to worry about anything; three square meals a day are provided, and I've got shelter over my head and a steady paycheck. I don't have to worry about what I'll do on any given day because I already know—I work. All decisions are made for me. The only thing I have to worry about is the possibility of dying.

✚

Going back to the real world is what scares me. Getting a job, paying the bills, putting food on the table; I will have to do that now that no one is giving it to me. Somebody tell me what to do?! I've been ordered around and can't stand it. I'm looking for the time where I call the shots—and I'm worried it could be worse. I'll have no one to blame but myself. Soon I'll no longer have to worry about death; now it's life I have to worry about. It's now time for me to be a man, and it's the scariest thing I'll ever do. It really scares me. It really scares me that I won't have what it takes. That's a scary thought.

MONTH 12

"THE GODDAMN ARMY MADE ME A MAN."

WEEK 1, DAY 6, IRAQ

0700 HOURS, OR

"Anthony, guess what the GOBs are up to now?" Torres yells as I open the door to the hospital. "They want us to look like the perfect unit that doesn't have everyone sleeping with each other. CSM Lavaled even went up to Cardoza and told her that we have to cool it.

"They're cracking down on couples. We're supposed to set a good example for the unit that's going to replace us. Do you believe that? After letting everyone do whatever they wanted for the past year, now they want to crack the whip so they can look good. They've got their bitch, CSM Lavaled, doing all of the dirty work."

Laveled has been making the rounds telling everyone to cool their jets, and everyone has been complying. That is until Lavaled comes across an officer in the pharmacy section named Captain Welch. He's six feet tall, 100 percent Scottish. He's also married and having an affair with a married woman, Colonel Gollen, who is an Asian doctor in the ICW.

"Excuse me, Sergeant Major Lavaled, stand at attention when you talk to me," Captain Welch yells. "Sergeant major, you are in charge of the enlisted for your section. What makes you think that you can give me an order? I am an officer. I take my orders from Colonel Jelly, not from some enlisted soldier."

Sergeant Major Lavaled is now standing erect at the position of attention.

"Sir, my orders are coming direct from Colonel Jelly," he replies.

"Sergeant Major, I don't think you understand the chain of command. If Colonel Jelly wants to give me an order he can do it himself. I don't need to follow orders given or relayed by you. Do you understand that?"

Sergeant Major Lavaled bites his lip. He's used to being in charge of enlisted soldiers and making everyone act subservient around him. Now he has to do the same to the officer.

Sergeant Major Lavaled goes straight back to Colonel Jelly's office. Jelly tells Lavaled to handle the problem with Welch and Gollen and to let them know it's a direct order from him. Lavaled pages Welch and Gollen, and they come to his office.

"I need to speak to you one at time please," Lavaled begins.

"I don't think so; you can speak to both of us at the same time," Welch retorts.

"Listen, sir, it is a direct order from Colonel Jelly."

"We don't need to talk to you," Gollen jumps in.

"Fine, whatever, I'll talk to you," Welch says and walks inside Command Sergeant Major Lavaled's office.

"I'm coming too then," Gollen protests, and follows Welch toward the office. Lavaled jumps in front of her and pushes her back, closing the door behind him. Stunned, Gollen stands there, and ten seconds later she opens the door to find Welch and Lavaled holding each other by their shirts, ready to hit one another.

"What are you two doing. . . ?" Gollen screams and grabs Welch by the arm and pulls him away.

WEEK 2, DAY 3, IRAQ

1700 HOURS, OR

"Hey Anthony, you heard about Sergeant Major Lavaled and Colonel Gollen?" Reto asks me as we wrap surgical tape around a broom handle and get ready for another day of indoor OR baseball.

"I heard about Lavaled and Welch almost getting into a fight. Is that what you're talking about?"

"Nah, man, haven't you noticed how Lavaled and Jelly haven't been around for a few days?"

"Yeah."

"It's because Lavaled is at a hearing in Baghdad. Gollen filed a sexual harassment claim against him saying that he showed her his penis."

"Haha, what are you talking about?"

"Well, apparently Gollen filed a complaint, and no one took it seriously because they had all heard about how she broke up a fight between Welch and Lavaled. She then went on record and said that Lavaled has a tattoo of Winnie-the-Pooh, slightly above and to the right of his penis."

"Winnie-the-Pooh?"

"True story, I swear. So once Gollen says this they check out Lavaled, and sure enough he's got the tattoo in the exact same spot she described. Winnie-the-Pooh in all his glory, and Gollen described it in detail, too, right down to the jar of honey."

"So what, they had sex or something?"

"No, man. Here's the best part. A few weeks ago, Lavaled was at the gym and he ran into Gollen. They started talking about abdominal muscles, and Lavaled lifted up his shirt to show off his abs. Gollen saw just the top of the tattoo. She asked him to pull down his shorts at an angle, so as to still cover his cock but show off the rest of the tattoo."

"That's insane."

"It's his word against hers."

WEEK 3, DAY 2, IRAQ

1100 HOURS, POST OFFICE

I grab my boxes and head to the post office. Send it home: movies, clothes, books, everything. On the way out I see Sergeant Cost coming in. She's got a cart full of fifteen large packages. I begin to wonder how much stuff she could actually have.

1130 HOURS, MY ROOM

"Hey, man, did you get all your stuff mailed out?" Torres asks me as I walk back into our room.

"Yeah I did, it was crazy. Sergeant Cost goes in there with like fifteen packages to send home."

"Were they on a cart and wrapped in white paper?"

"Yeah."

"She did that yesterday, too, a cart full of packages—"

Torres and I begin discussing all the different possibilities of what she could be mailing home in all of those packages.

"You guys talking about Cost?" Markham is saying.

"Yeah."

"You know, I was at the post office three days ago and, I'm not even kidding, she was mailing like twenty packages home. I was curious what she was mailing home so I ask around the hospital. You know those Soldier's Angels packages we're always getting?"

Torres and I nod our heads.

Soldier's Angels is a group of caring and concerned citizens who send supplies to the soldiers overseas. Throughout the year, we've received hundreds and hundreds of packages from them that we keep with the other surplus goods: soaps, shampoos, candy, cookies, razors, lotions, anything and everything.

"So I asked around," Markham says as he picks up his guitar and begins to play. "And it turns out she's been saving all of the Solider's Angels packages she's received throughout the year here. She's sending them home so that she won't have to buy anything for years. She's raided the surplus supply room at the post office, too."

WEEK 4, DAY 5, IRAQ

1100 HOURS, OR

The unit that is replacing us is all finally here. Colonel Reke and Gagney are giving the soldiers a tour as well as their commander, sergeant major, and a handful of colonels. In the OR break room, me, Reto, Torres, Denti, Chandler, Hudge, Elster, Sellers, Waters, and Cather are standing around, I suppose saying goodbye. It's our last day here. Colonel Reke and Gagney bring the tour past us;

we're all talking and having fun with each other. The soldiers from the new unit ask us questions. Reto grabs two Snapples out of the refrigerator. He hands one to me and pops the top off of the one for himself, reading the fun little fact that's printed on the inside of the cap. Across the room, Gagney sees him and wants to show Reke and all the other colonels that he's friends with his troops. He yells across the room, "Hey Reto, what does the cap say?" The room goes silent. Pleased that everyone is paying attention to him—and how hip he looks in front of the other soldiers—Gagney, and everyone, wait patiently as Reto reads out the fact:

"On average a human will spend up to two weeks kissing in his/her lifetime."

Gagney, looking to take his coolness up a notch, says, "Wow, ha ha, I guess I've already had more than my lifetime's worth of kissing. Hell, I'll do that my first month back." There are a few stifled laughs, and you can smell the awkwardness in the air. Suddenly, like a bolt of lightning, I get a brilliant idea. It might get me in trouble, but I just don't care. It's too perfect, I've got to do it . . . I might get in trouble. . . .

I've got to say it, quick, before the moment passes. . . . Patience. . . . Wait for the right moment. . . . Now! Go! Say it!

"I think they mean kissing someone on the lips, not on the ass."

A few seconds pass in silence. Everyone looks at each other and takes in the comment. Then the entire room bursts into gutwrenching laughter; all the colonels (even Reke) start laughing, and, of course, Reto and I do, too. After seeing everyone else, Gagney tries to fake a laugh.

Gagney's power over us is gone, and now those with actual character and personality are back in charge.

Tomorrow we leave for Kuwait, then Wisconsin for a week to do out-processing, and then we leave to go back home—for good.

THE LAST DAY

0900 HOURS, FLIGHT HOME

"I think I'm going to be sick," says Reto.

Our entire unit, both the northern and southern hospitals, are on one plane ride home, and Reto comes by to tell me what he just heard.

"Why, what's up?" I say.

"So I was in my seat sitting behind Sergeant Blett, and she was sitting with Hikenski and Travis and they were all telling each other how they can't wait to be home with their husband and kids."

"They've been cheating on their husbands this entire time!"

"They were all laughing and crying," Reto says.

"This is fucking incredible. They acted like they could have cared less about their families while they were here, now they're all giddy about seeing them. I fucking hate people."

"I'll go back to my seat. It looks like Denti wants to sit here."

"No, stay here. I don't want fucking Denti sitting here again. I had to sit with him the entire first part of the flight," but Reto ignores me.

0915 HOURS, FLIGHT HOME

When Denti sits down next to me, I see a pillow go flying across the aisle, then another one, then another one. A minute later almost the entire plane is throwing pillows around and having a giant pillow fight. I look at them all and I see everyone smiling and laughing and having a good time. None of them seem like the people I've just spent a year with. I begin to feel nostalgic. These are my brothers and sisters. We've shared a journey that few people in the world will ever know about, much less be able to relate to.

1015 HOURS, FLIGHT HOME

The plane makes a stopover in Germany, where it refuels, and then we get back onto the plane. The entire stopover consisted of me yelling at Denti: "No, that's a bidet, not a water bubbler. . . ."

"Hey, smell my breath," Denti says as we get back on the plane.

"What? I'm not going to smell your breath; go sit somewhere else," I reply.

"No. Me and this guy stole some nips of absinthe out of the gift shop. I feel all warm and tingly. Hey, man, do you want to play cards? We can play poker, Rummy 500. Do you want to watch a movie on my DVD player? Do you want to sit here and talk? I can't believe we're almost home. I can't wait."

I begin to notice why absinthe is illegal in the States. Not because it has a high level of toxicity and can make people hallucinate, but because it makes people annoying as fuck. "Denti, shut up. I'm trying to go to sleep."

"Hey, man, let me get some of your Ambien. You have like a whole bag left; let me get one."

"I'm not going to give you a whole one."

"Fine, whatever; give me something so I'll just pass out."

I give Denti half (approximately 5 mg) of an Ambien pill.

1025 HOURS, FLIGHT HOME

"Hey, man, I'm not tired. I'm wired. Give me another half a pill. This shit isn't working," says Denti.

"Listen! It takes twenty minutes to a half-hour to kick in. Just wait."

Denti then proceeds to poke my arm. "Come on, man, give me another half one . . . come on."

"Fine, but that's it. Wait for it to kick in."

1035 HOURS, FLIGHT HOME

"Hey, man, this shit sucks. I'm still wide awake. Give me another full pill and I promise I'll leave you alone."

"Denti, seriously, shut the fuck up; I'm trying to sleep."

"I swear, man, give me one more. A full pill and I'll shut up. This shit doesn't even work. Just give me one more; I'm buzzed, man. All I want to do is sleep. Come on . . . come on . . . come on. . . ."

"All right, Denti, but if you ask one more time, I'm going to suffocate you with my miniature airplane pillow."

I give Denti the final pill, and he gulps it down. He now has had two nips of absinthe and 20 mg of Ambien. Finally I get some peace and quiet and can try and go to sleep.

He's out for the next four hours. Then his body begins shaking and his arms are in the air like a T-Rex. I'm not sure if all the Ambien and absinthe is a deadly mix and I begin worrying.

What the fuck should I do? Should I get someone and ask for help? Should I tell them about the absinthe and Ambien? What should I do? What should I do? He could die.

Or then again, he could be totally fine.

Maybe nothing will happen. I should just close my eyes and go to sleep. If anyone walks by and sees him I can just say I don't know what happened, I was sleeping.

Whatever, he'll be fine . . . just go to sleep.

OUT-PROCESSING, FT. McCOY, WISCONSIN

1500 HOURS, AUDITORIUM

We are doing out-processing. It consists of filling out paper-work and telling people that we won't kill ourselves. We officially fly home tomorrow, but tonight we are having a big awards ceremony. Most everyone is getting one of two awards, the Army Achievement Medal or the Army Accommodation Medal.

Colonel Jelly is onstage shaking hands and handing out the awards. One of the GOBs is reading out the names of everyone and what award they will be getting. Some people are also receiving Bronze Stars. A Bronze Star is the fifth-highest award that any person can receive in the United States military.

By the time the night ends, fifty Bronze Stars are handed out. The recipients include men and women (officers) who were having adulterous affairs and nominating each other for awards. Award winners also include all of the GOBs, Colonel Jelly, Captain Dillon, Staff Sergeant North, and Command Sergeant Major Lavaled. As some of the names are called for the Bronze Stars, boos can be heard throughout the auditorium.

But none of it matters to me, I'll tell you what matters to me: I survived a war; I survived a year outside of my comfort zone without any friends or family. The goddamn Army made me a man.

EPILOGUE

It's been almost two years since I left Iraq. While I don't see many of the other soldiers I lived with for a year, I hear about them often.

✛

Sergeant Hudge finished up her contract, left the Army, and just had her first baby. She and her husband are now in the middle of a divorce.

Specialist Denti and Sergeant Elster finished up their contracts and left the army. Sergeant Elster finally admitted that he was the one throwing the shitty toilet paper into the trash. (In Iraq, toilet paper is not used. The plumbing system cannot handle it—so Iraqis use their hands. Whether he was afraid to test the facilities or he was just playing with our minds, we may never know.)

Specialist Torres and Sergeant Cardoza are now living together.

Specialist Markham is married and works at Home Depot. We are currently trying to sell a screenplay he wrote while in Iraq.

Staff Sergeant Clementine and Specialist Proust got married and moved to Louisiana. They got divorced a few months later.

Sergeant Sellers left the Army and is battling a drug problem.

Specialist Reto is an operating room technician in Maine.

Staff Sergeant Gagney signed up to be a trainer for units being deployed to Iraq.

First Sergeant Mardine retired from the army.

Staff Sergeant Blett came clean and told her husband about the affair she had with Pyne while in Iraq.

Currently there is a lawsuit against Fort McCoy in Wisconsin for the horrible living and food conditions.

Sadly, Specialist Crade took his own life. When I first heard the news, I felt empty. And then the anger rose in me. At the same time I heard about Crade, I heard Colonel Jelly had been promoted to General.

ABOUT THE AUTHOR

SPC Michael Anthony seemed destined to serve from the day he was born. The youngest of seven children, Anthony has four brothers and two sisters, all of whom joined the military (except for one sister). His father and two grandfathers were also in the military.

After graduation from high school, he went to basic training and then job training to become an operating room medic. One year later he returned home and enrolled in college to begin his first semester. Almost immediately upon finishing his first semester he was shipped off to Wisconsin to train for four months before he would leave and spend his next year in Iraq. Since returning home, Anthony is working on his next book, and toward a bachelor's degree in creative writing. He lives in Massachusetts.

Anthony is being featured in Erik Spink's documentary about the invisible wounds of war. You can contact Anthony and find links to the documentary through his website, *www.MassCasualties.com*.